THIRD EDITION

P9-CKE-296

LIFE BY PERSONAL DESIGN

Realizing Your Dream

MARIA NAPOLI, PhD
SUE ROE, DPA

Kendall Hunt
publishing company

Kendall Hunt
publishing company

www.kendallhunt.com
Send all inquiries to:
4050 Westmark Drive
Dubuque, IA 52004-1840

CONTENTS

ABOUT THE AUTHORS

Dr. Sue Roe is the principal member of The Roe Group Enterprises, LLC. Her professional career focuses on expert and process consultation in the areas of workforce and professional competencies and development, assessment and evaluation, and instructional design and development. Her company offers continuing education as well as e-guidebooks on special topics in holistic health, business, and education.

Dr. Roe has diverse administrative experience in both private and public sector institutions and has keynoted and been a presenter at a variety of conventions, seminars, workshops, and programs across the country. Dr. Roe has taught and designed academic courses for over 35 years at several public and private universities and colleges using a variety of delivery formats.

She is co-author of a recently published allied health textbook and a textbook on holistic nursing. She is currently co-authoring a textbook on leadership in healthcare. She is the co-chapter leader for the Arizona chapter of the American Holistic Nurses Association and is a member of the Review Panel for the Journal of Holistic Nursing. She is also the Executive Editor of "Wholistic Now!" a quarterly online newsletter that features multi-disciplinary perspectives on integrative health, wellness, and the delivery of holistic healthcare.

Dr. Roe has received awards for her professional leadership activities and has served on several community and professional Boards of Directors and quality and credentialing committees. She developed and was the executive director of a consortium which focused on complementary/alternative medicine.

She has a doctorate in public administration with an emphasis in administration and health policy with additional graduate work in educational administration and instructional design and development. She also has a Master of Science and a Bachelor of Science degree in Nursing.

Dr. Roe is a highly respected professional, community leader, skillful facilitator, and a dynamic change agent.

Maria Napoli is an associate professor at Arizona Sate University. She has incorporated the practice of mindfulness in research, teaching, trainings and presentations at conferences nationally and internationally. She has developed mindfulness programs for elementary school children, undergraduate and graduate students including a graduate certificate in integrative health with a focus on mindfulness practice. It is her vision to bring mindfulness into education at all levels with the intention of supporting students to perform at their personal best with empathy and focus on quality of life. She has published journal articles and five books: *A Family Casebook: Problem Based Learning and Mindful Self Reflection; Tools for Mindful Living: Practicing the Four Step MAC Guide; Beyond Stress: Strategies for Blissful Living; Whole Person Health: Mindful Living Across the Lifespan* (with Steve Peterson); and *Sustainable Living and Mindful Eating* (with Lisa Schmidt) (co-created CD with Susan Busatti-Giangano).

PROLOGUE

The journey in which you are about to embark in *Life by Personal Design: Realizing your Dream* can result in creating the *life you love*. For some their lives may need improvements, and for others they may require a complete makeover! What you may need to achieve the *life you love* is yet for you to discover. The important principle when reading and integrating the insights you gain from *Life by Personal Design* is that there are no limits to the changes you can make to realize your dreams. Take the time to personally explore and experience the many new horizons you will find in this book and benefit from the life-changing self-reflective and interactive activities that can help you attain greater happiness and success.

As you begin your journey, think about your lifelong personal values and strategies. Some of these may no longer serve you and are not useful; others you may choose to keep. Throughout your travels in *Life by Personal Design: Realizing your Dream,* you will examine your strategies. In each chapter you will have a decision to make: shall I keep, add to, and/ or remove my personal lifelong strategies? By doing this you will create ways to improve your life. You will become aware of what you are willing to do and actions you will take to make changes. You will also

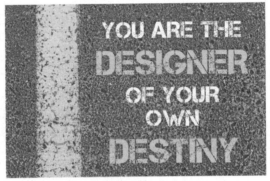

discover what obstacles may be in your way. *Life by Personal Design* is unique. It offers you an integrated perspective and gives YOU personal control to create your unique life design to realize the *life you love*.

You start your journey with *Mindfully Creating the Life You Love*. When you are mindful, you pay attention to experiences without judgment. You become aware! By practicing mindfulness there is no confusion about what is occurring in your life. You are completely engaged in the moment—not looking back or ahead and not "stuck" in old thinking and behavior patterns. When you are living in the present you clear the path to practice gratitude, compassion, self-forgiveness, and forgiveness of others. Approaching your life mindfully opens up a panorama of choices and actions you can take; ones you may have never seen before.

In *Eating with Joy and Harmony,* you explore the intimate relationship you have with the food you eat, the joy it can create, and the harmony it can have with your body. You examine not only what you eat, but identify your preferred eating patterns, the foods you select, and how certain foods make you feel both physically and emotionally. You look at what draws you to certain foods and how food can provide you with energy or can make you feel lethargic. Paying attention to what and how you eat (eating mindfully) is one of the greatest gifts you can give yourself.

In *Maximizing Your Body's Vitality,* you have a chance to go beyond the idea of thinking about your body as simply being composed of muscles, ligaments, tendons, and bones. Bodies are "mean energy machines" with the ability to endure years of abuse from lack of exercise, poor eating habits, and stress. While all of us need some form of physical activity, different bodies have different needs and function at different energy levels. Finding the exercise, energy work, and recreational activities that will work in your life and meets your body's needs is surely the way to build its vitality.

In *Discovering Your Balance: Rest and Relaxation* you are reminded about the need to nurture yourself. Finding ways to feel rested, creating opportunities for relaxation, and getting healthful sleep are essential to maintaining balance. These are often forgotten in the rush of the day where there is little time to rest, relax, or sleep resulting in increased stress and, for some, insomnia which, over time, can be harmful to your body. One day you may find yourself asking the question: where has all my time gone? Remember, you cannot take time back, but you can make rest, relaxation, and sleep an integral part of how you spend your time and life.

In *Building Harmonious Relationships,* you find a mirror to self-reflect on how you are impacted by the significant others in your life. Understanding how you developed your relationships with people can be an uphill climb when you factor in changes that occur in those relationships over time. Exploring how to improve your relationships, managing any conflicts you may have, and identifying the relationships that may hold you back from transforming your life to one you *love* are key ingredients to greater fulfillment.

In *Protecting Your Life Space: Environmental Awareness,* you will increase your ecological awareness of your home, work, and community. Living in a chemical-and pollutant-free environment is the goal. Simple changes such as maintaining effective hand hygiene, drinking water from stainless-steel bottles instead of plastic, reducing the amount of time you use a microwave, to airing out your bed daily to prevent mites from breeding are just a few ways to become environmentally aware. You have control in more ways than you know to make safer and healthier choices in your living environment.

In *Cherishing Your Passions,* you examine what "makes you tick." You will ask yourself: Am I in a rut? Are things too routine? Am I acting on "shoulds" rather than wants? Am I lacking joy or happiness in my life? You may reflect on: Am I moving through my life without direction? Or am I not really focusing on what I really want to do? The hope is that when your journey reaches this far into *Life by Personal Design,* you are more able to fully and mindfully answer these questions because you will be ready to create the *life you love*!

In *Visioning Your Life,* you are now prepared to set intention in your life. You have the resilience needed and are willing to move forward on what you want to have happen. You have insight into how to remove the obstacles that may get in your way. You know what you have to do to engage in and live your personal vision. And, you feel excited and energized about creating the *life you love*!

We are delighted to share *Life by Personal Design: Realizing Your Dream.* We encourage you to take advantage of the many opportunities found in this book. Be sure to pursue the self-reflective and interactive activities found at the end of each chapter. These include the 4 Step MAC Guide, Designer Activities, Life by Personal Design Reflective Journal, Readings of Interest, and References.

MINDFULNESS PRACTICE USING THE MINDFUL MAC GUIDE

The Mindful MAC Guide helps you practice mindfulness by:

1. Empathically **acknowledging** each experience without internal or external filters
2. Intentionally paying **attention** to your senses, thoughts, emotions, and instincts regarding each experience
3. **Accepting** your experience without judgment or expectations
4. **Choosing** to respond versus react to your experience

DESIGNER ACTIVITIES

The Designer Activities provide you with an opportunity to "try out" experiences related to what you learned in the chapter. This will assist you in determining whether you choose to modify or perhaps add to your personal lifelong strategies.

LIFE BY PERSONAL DESIGN REFLECTIVE JOURNAL

The Reflective Journal for each chapter offers a consistent place for you to record what you learned from the chapter, the resulting "intentions" for change, any barriers you think might interfere with these desired changes and how you will overcome them, and at least *one* strategy that will help you realize your dreams and the life you will love.

READINGS OF INTEREST AND REFERENCES

Readings of Interest are complementary resources that offer additional articles, or websites that you may want to pursue further. References support the research and practice based information found in the chapter.

Before you launch into *Life by Personal Design*, it is important to complete the ***Quality of Life Self Care Wheel—Reflection and Discovery.*** You can find the Inventory and more information about the 7 Dimensions of the Wheel on the following pages. Look at the 7 Dimensions of the Wheel. These include health, rest and recreation, personal development and relationships, finances, the environment, career/school, and passion. Think about how well you are functioning in each.

Review the Dimensions of the Quality of Life Self Care Wheel found on this Inventory.

Think about how each Dimension relates to you. Then select a number from 10 High to 1 Low which best reflects your level of realizing this Dimension. Look at your score for each Dimension. If it is a 10 or close to it this means you have fantastic balance and wellness. If it is closer to 5 or below this means you need to consider an adjustment in your life. As you read *Life by Personal Design* remember these scores so you can use them as you complete chapter activities and as a basis for your "intentions" for change.

When you complete the ***Quality of Life Self Care Wheel—Reflection and Discovery*** Inventory, you are ready to start chapter 1. When you finish reading this book and completing the activities and Journals, you will find the ***Quality of Life Self Care Wheel—Plan for Intention and Action*** to assist you in taking next steps.

We are confident that this journey you are about to embark on will help you discover ways to improve and enhance the quality of your life. Our wish is for you to have days filled with fun, meaning, and health, but, most of all, our desire is for you to personally design and live the *life you love*.

Maria and Sue

QUALITY OF LIFE SELF CARE WHEEL REFLECTION AND DISCOVERY

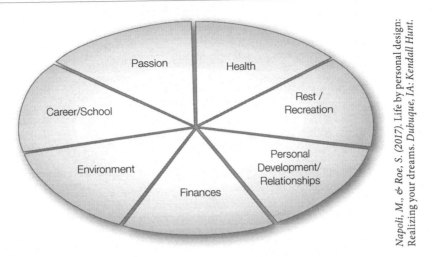

Napoli, M., & Roe, S. (2017). Life by personal design: Realizing your dreams. Dubuque, IA: Kendall Hunt.

Instructions: Review the Dimensions of the Quality of Life Self Care Wheel. Think about how each Dimension relates to you. Then select a number from 10 High to 1 Low which best reflects your level of realizing the Dimension.

DIMENSION	QUALITY OF LIFE SCALE—PLEASE CIRCLE
	10 = HIGH TO 1 = LOW
Health	10 9 8 7 (6) 5 4 3 2 1
Rest/Recreation	10 9 8 7 (6) 5 4 3 2 1
Personal Development/Relationships	10 9 8 7 (6) 5 4 3 2 1
Finances	10 9 8 7 6 5 4 3 2 (1)
Environment	10 9 (8) 7 6 5 4 3 2 1
Career/School	10 9 8 7 (6) 5 4 3 2 1
Passion	10 9 8 (7) 6 5 4 3 2 1

WHAT DOES YOUR SCORE MEAN:

10–9: Fantastic Balance/Wellness   **8–7:** Good Job

6: Doing Okay   **5 and Below:** Needs Adjustment

QUALITY OF LIFE SELF CARE WHEEL REFLECTION AND DISCOVERY DIMENSIONS—SOME EXAMPLES

Health: Healthful eating, exercising, maintaining an appropriate weight, regular physical exams, and using effective stress reduction strategies.

Rest/Recreation: Adequate sleep and rest periods, interspersing work with play, pursuing hobbies, realizing happiness, and having fun.

Personal Development/Relationships: Fulfilling and rewarding relationships with others in your life, needed emotional support systems, developing personal goals such as improving listening, and having meaning and purpose through a desired spiritual life.

Finances: Sufficient resources to support self and those responsible for, aligning needed resources with daily requirements, and adequate discretionary income to purchase wanted items.

Environment: Awareness and being respectful of the environment in which you live in and those around you, having sensitivity to the impact you have on the environment, being chemical/pollutant free, recycling, and using natural products.

Career/School: Regularly improving your knowledge and skill base, setting professional goals and achieving them, having a satisfying and meaningful profession/occupation, being content with your work life, and pursuing work life balance.

Passion: Understanding, defining, and living your life based on your inner feelings, desires, and dreams.

CHAPTER 1

MINDFULLY CREATING THE LIFE YOU LOVE

© Maria Napoli

Photo courtesy of Marie Napoli

Life is a panorama of experiences
Embrace the challenges
Take risks
Dream big

(Napoli)

LEARN TO MINDFULLY CREATE THE LIFE YOU LOVE

- Make mindfulness a part of your daily life
- Practice self-compassion
- Increase your capacity for self-forgiveness
- Integrate and express gratitude
- Have a purpose in life
- Use the Mindful MAC Guide to improve your ability to be present

© charles taylor/Shutterstock.com

When you wake up in the morning, much of your time before you even leave the house may be focused on thoughts and activities that are outer-directed such as work, chores, and schedules. How often do you wake, take stock of yourself, maybe look in the mirror, pat yourself on the back, and acknowledge what an amazing person you are? Or, are you more outer-directed and focus only on work, chores, and schedules? Taking this one step further, how often do you congratulate yourself for the selfless acts you do? Do you breathe in gratitude for the good things you do for yourself as well as others, and even forgive yourself for decisions you regret making?

When you choose a mindful life you give yourself the opportunity to create the "life you love" by becoming more inner-directed. Imagine you are a seed, and every day you water the seed with self-care, compassion, gratitude, and forgiveness. Before you know it, you are blooming like a beautiful flower, vibrant, and exquisite to see and feel.

Mindfulness is described as the acceptance of moment-to-moment experiences without internal or external filters. When your internal mindless chatter is listened to, it stimulates you, pushing you back into the past or propelling you toward the future taking you out of the present moment. This is when you are no longer mindful.

Snapshots

Cartoonstock.com

"I don't get it. I play in the park, eat all day long, get back rubs from strangers, and still I wonder, 'What's it all about?'"

From birth your perceptions of the world around you are shaped by the interactions of significant people in your life. You are influenced by the adults and children you engage with to survive and to satisfy your social and emotional needs. As you mature, the capacity to meet your own needs in a loving kind way help create the life you love.

How do you get there? The first step is to think about how you passed through life without noticing the obvious; letting precious opportunities drift away without awareness. Unfortunately, one reason this happens is that when people enter the world they do it mindfully but then take an about face into mindlessness. First encounters and everyday situations are mindful, however, as people increase their interactions they gradually seem to decrease being present, frequently getting caught in the past or having expectations about the future. There are probably many reasons for this, such as being stuck in "fight or flight" from stress, adhering to the norms of family and society, or trying to meet the expectations of others.

Let's explore the cycle of moving from mindfulness to mindlessness and then revisit how to move back to living a mindful life.

For infants, mindfulness is inherent in everyday communication with the internal and outside world. Infants listen to body cues of hunger, pain, need for touch, and instincts. They are integrally connected to their experiences whether they are comfortable or uncomfortable; they all matter. When people are mindful they pay attention to their environment; the smells, tastes, sight, hearing, smiles and frowns, good and bad touch, happy and sad emotions, and the energy around them. Before language is even learned, infants begin to mirror and internalize the non-verbal emotions and experiences of their caregivers. The reality is that people can reconnect with these basic experiences when they are mindful. It is no surprise that adults often wish to be a child again, reflecting upon the feeling "oh, to be free as a child again without a care in the world." In actuality, as children it is full engagement of experiences, comfortable and uncomfortable, that gives freedom. So, what happens? Why do people get stuck? Unfortunately, in the modern world infants move quickly from being mindful into mindlessness as they enter childhood.

Snapshots

"I understand *how* I was born; I want to know *why*."

Cartoonstock.com

As infants develop and enter early childhood the privilege of embracing the world on their own terms begins to change. Children soon feel rejection and judgment of family and social norms, which can take them out of their mindful experience and into others' expectations of what is acceptable. Thus, children begin to repress feelings to gain approval from others. As children move along the developmental timeline, they learn to conform, and exhibit emotions and behaviors to meet the approval of adults. By the time they reach adolescence children are stuck in mindlessness. Of course with guidance, they can replace the adult world of mindlessness where restriction, judgments, expectations, and autocratic discipline occur more frequently than choice, acceptance, and interactive discussion. The spontaneous developmental behavioral and emotional spurts during adolescence are often frowned upon, placing adolescents in a "box" where they must rebel to be free. To prevent judgment of adolescent behavior it can be helpful to teach mindfulness skills to help with emotional regulation in a positive way.

As adults, experience with the outside world and the many roles people have increases dependence on language and social norms. This can impede acknowledging and accepting these experiences without judgment. Paying attention to the senses, body language and instincts, which came easily as children, are important cues to understand the nuances of experiences. A study using body movement and gestures as cues to emotions in younger and older adults found that younger adults had fewer errors in identifying emotions expressed than the older adults [1] The result shows that as people get older they pay less attention to emotional experiences. To note, mindfulness increases the ability to be non-judgmental thereby increasing the capacity to experience emotions in a more positive way. Even uncomfortable moments are valuable, helping people grow into evolved human beings. Repressing and avoiding experiences limit and take up unnecessary space in life. What happens is these thoughts and emotions are given permission to haunt you over and over again. The repetitive reacting to emotions rather than responding to them is the anchor that keeps people from moving past these emotions and creating the life they love. As you develop emotional intelligence you are better equipped to deal with life's challenges.

© conrado/Shutterstock.com

Emotionally intelligent individuals have been shown to be more resilient and better able to adapt to change under stress. They see stress as a challenge versus a threat.[2] One might predict that being able to meet life's challenges can be an important influence in creating the "life you love." You would not be stuck or afraid to move through difficult situations. A meta-analysis of 25 studies concluded that those who perceive, know, and manage their emotions might deal better with emotional issues and as a result experience greater psychological well-being.[3] When you can accept joy and suffering you are better able to accept it in others. Opening the doors to give and receive love is enhanced by being mindful, as there is more space for acceptance and the door on judgment is more easily closed. Non-judgment is one of the most valuable gifts you can give yourself to increase the quality of your life and to help you realize your dreams. When you are mindful, you open up the opportunity to be a non-judgmental witness to your present experience. The result is CHOICE. When you pay attention to your experience you have a CHOICE to *do something or do nothing*. You have the privilege of accepting each experience granted in life, whether or not your present experience elicits positive or negative thoughts and emotions. You have the CHOICE to react or respond.

Through your acceptance of experiences you carve out a path for happiness. How you "show up" will determine the outcome. The more time you spend accepting your moment-to-moment experiences without judgment the greater opportunity you will have for genuine happiness. To help you learn how to do this, review the following Mindful MAC Guide:

Mindful **MAC** Guide

acknowledge
attention
accept
choose

1. Empathically acknowledge each experience without internal or external filters
2. Intentionally pay attention to your senses, thoughts, emotions, and instincts regarding each experience
3. Accept your experience without judgment or expectations
4. Choose to respond versus react to your experience.[4]

Enjoy your first experience with the Mindful MAC Guide by focusing on your breath.

Close your eyes and bring your attention to your breath. Notice the rise of your belly on the inhale and its fall on exhale.

- *Acknowledge* all aspects of the breathing experience by noticing the rhythm of your breath
- *Pay Attention* to your senses, thoughts, emotions and instincts regarding your breathing experience. You may notice shallow, rapid, short, or deep breathing.
- *Accept* your breathing experience without judgment. Now gently open your eyes and look around you. What do you notice? Take in this awareness.
- *Choose* how you would like to proceed with your breathing experience.

You can do this simple activity daily to begin to stay in the moment and bring mindfulness into your life. The breath is your life source, taking its direction by how your life is lived. You may notice that your breath is short when anxious, rapid when fearful, and sometimes it stops when in shock or feeling aghast. This gift of life, breath, is your ticket to living a mindful life. Paying attention to your breath does not take up extra time, cost any money, and does not involve the cooperation of anyone other than yourself. It offers a multitude of bonuses that add quality to your life. This is the best deal you will ever have. Take it! The fact is you only have today, this moment, and this second, so why not embrace it.

Now that that developmental milestones have been discussed and you can see the influence they have, let's look at how you, as an adult, can navigate a direction toward creating the life you love. Remember, people, events, and circumstances will always impact you, yet when you develop emotional intelligence and practice mindfulness, you have a good chance of creating the life you love.

When you live mindfully you gain the capacity to master self-compassion, gratitude, and forgiveness. An important tenet of mindfulness is non-judgment so when you practice self-compassion, you can free yourself of emotional pain that can be a roadblock to personal growth. Self-compassion has been conceptualized as self-kindness, common humanity, and mindfulness.[5] People are all perfect in their imperfections and outcomes of decisions often stimulate self-doubt and criticism. When you are self-compassionate you can reflect upon your imperfections and simply acknowledge that decisions made are lessons to be cherished and opportunities to move forward. Think about the precious time saved if you were able to have more self-compassion. You are not alone with events that occur in your life. Many people have also experienced failure, rejection, and humiliation, which may lessen the investment in holding onto painful experiences.

SELF COMPASSION

© hafakot/Shutterstock.com

It is important to note the difference between self-compassion and self esteem. Self-esteem is related to how a person perceives self-worth and social approval, which can be seen as narcissistic where self-compassion is not evaluative. Self-compassion relates to self, acknowledging, "we are imperfect human beings who experience suffering and are therefore worthy of compassion"[6] Research has shown that self-esteem has a positive association with narcissism whereas the association between self-compassion and narcissism was close to zero.[7] One might say that those who are self-compassionate are less narcissistic as they embrace their weaknesses as well as their strengths creating more emotional balance. It has also been found that those who experienced increased self-compassion also experienced increased social connectedness and decreased self-criticism, depression, rumination, thought suppression, and anxiety.[8] Since self-compassion is associated with acknowledging suffering as a human experience, it might be said that those who are self-compassionate are less likely to dwell on their sorrows.

© Andrey_I/Shutterstock.com

Many people experience loneliness at one time or another. Those who often feel lonely may not look favorably upon themselves, increasing the propensity for extended periods of loneliness. A study of university students and self-compassion and loneliness found that self-compassion ingredients of self-kindness, common humanity, and mindfulness were negatively related to loneliness. On the other hand, self-judgment, isolation, and over-identification were associated with loneliness.[9] Although most people experience loneliness to some degree, when they are mindful and practice self-compassion through non-judgment, they are open to interconnection with others and can decrease the time spent feeling lonely. A study of Japanese individuals who had low self-compassion significantly improved their self-kindness from pre-treatment to post-treatment following an intervention of being kind to themselves. Taking cultural implications into consideration where self-compassion is generally lower and self-criticism is higher in this population, the effective intervention of increasing self-compassion is relevant showing the strength of practicing self-compassion.[10]

When you are self-compassionate you reflect upon your experiences just as they are without filtering them through social norms or expectations. In regard to mindfulness, when people are self-compassionate, they acknowledge their emotions without holding on to them or letting their emotions control the experience. When you are mindful, self-compassion can be a resource to confront and understand negative emotions and reactions to them with objectivity and perspective instead of being swept away by the story line of your own pain.[11] Mindfulness is then viewed as a core ingredient of self-compassion and being mindful of your feelings is key to giving you compassion.[12] Accepting humanness with its imperfections is food for removing obstacles toward creating the life you love.

Many carry an imaginary gavel around dishing out sentences of guilt for perceived wrong doings. Can you forgive yourself if you feel you have wronged someone? "The first step toward self-forgiveness is to acknowledge that the behavior was wrong and accept responsibility for the behavior."[13] A key factor in practicing self-forgiveness is letting go of guilt. Results of a study with undergraduate students who were asked if they had done something hurtful and regrettable to another person within the past three days found that increases in guilt were associated with less self-forgiveness.[14] In a later study of undergraduates, students were asked to recall an event in the past two years in which they had offended someone by what they did or said. Results of this study found that guilt strongly impacted self-forgiveness.[15]

Self-forgiveness may be one of the most important ingredients in creating the life you love. As you begin to reflect upon your capacity for self-compassion and self-forgiveness you will realize that storing negative feelings and self-judging are truly roadblocks toward creating the life your love.

Let's turn to another aspect of enhancing your capacity for living the highest quality of life: gratitude. You may often find yourself in negative self-talk, thinking about the past and holding onto expectations of others and yourself. The simple act of gratitude has a multitude of benefits and without a doubt must be integrated into your toolbox of meaningful life acts. In its simplest form, gratitude is your appreciation of what you perceive as valuable and meaningful. Much of the research on gratitude has shown that those who practice gratitude have an increased sense of happiness and well-being. Research with college students found a significant correlation between gratitude and well-being.[16, 17, 18] Gratitude was also associated with greater life satisfaction for adolescents.[19] "Experiencing gratitude, thankfulness, and appreciation tends to foster positive feelings, which in turn contribute to one's overall sense of well-being."[20]

There are many ways to integrate gratitude into your overall lifestyle and the benefits are long lasting. Improving physical health and relationships, enhancing empathy and reducing aggression, improving sleep and self-esteem as well as decreasing the effects of trauma and increasing mental strength are some of these benefits.[21] When you wake up each morning, find one thing to be grateful for before you start your day. In relating to others, remember to express gratitude to one person every day. Both of these activities will take less than a minute. You can increase your happiness in only a few minutes a day. Imagine that!

myself
others

Having meaning in your life is another step toward creating the life you love. When you think about creating that life it is important to consider what enhances meaning in life. Meaning in life has been defined as making sense of and integrating experiences so that there is a clear understanding of oneself. It is also having purpose by actively pursuing goals that reflect one's identity beyond self-interest and feeling connected to something larger than oneself. Interesting to note a study of university students who reported a higher use of positive emotion words had more emotion suppression at follow-up. One might conclude that being positive all the time does not dictate happiness. Rather, being mindful may be a better predictor of happiness. When a person is mindful there is attention and focus on all events, not only the positive, thus creating more meaning in life and balance. Subsequently there would likely be less suppression of negative emotions.[22] Therefore, there can be many interpretations, and yet, in general, one may speculate that prosocial acts are key in having meaning in life while also enjoying the benefits of happiness; a result of prosocial behavior. Acts of gratitude is one prosocial action.

Other ways to experience meaning is having purpose, being connected to something bigger than yourself, and feeling that you matter and can have a positive impact on others. Research has found that prosocial behavior as measured by general altruistic behavior such as volunteering, and expressing gratitude by writing gratitude notes is related to enhancing meaning in life.[23] Does having purpose in life enhance well-being and meaning? When you commit to purpose in life you can ask yourself, "Where am I going?" This may entail setting goals and aspirations. Having purpose in life has been shown to predict well-being, a more positive self-image, and personality traits such as being more conscientious, agreeable, emotionally stable, extroverted, and open to new experiences.[24]

Keep in mind that experiencing the good life is different for each person and more so for those in various cultures. People from various cultures define their own meaning of what constitutes happiness. Research with Italian immigrants identified family relations, cultural affinity with Italy, geographical proximity to Italy, and the type of work where one was employed to shaping optimal experiences. Eastern Europeans and Indians had higher optimal experiences when they found work that allowed for professional development, relational or cultural competence, and connections. African immigrants who had employment opportunities that restricted professional development reported lower levels of optimal experience.[25] A sense of meaning and optimal experience related to purpose in life. "Where am I going?" is a strong indicator of success for not only being employed but for work satisfaction, which can have different meanings depending upon the culture in which one lives.

As you reflect upon your life, consider how you can create the life you love. There are so many aspects to your life; family, friends, work, school, neighbors, community, personal characteristics, passions, desires, imperfections, talents, physical ability, and personality to name a few. When you take a closer look at yourself, you may now understand that there are some key factors that will guide you to the best possible life you can have; one that you love. Read through the rest of this book, work through the activities, and begin practicing mindfulness. Don't wait. Start your creative path today!

MINDFULNESS PRACTICE
USING THE MINDFUL MAC GUIDE

Mindful **MAC** Guide

1. Mindfully **acknowledge** each experience without internal or external filters
2. Intentionally pay **attention** to your senses, thoughts, emotions, and instincts regarding each experience
3. **Accept** your experience without judgment or expectations
4. **Choose** to respond versus react to your experience

I notice I live in the past or ruminate about things that have happened. Describe.

It's difficult for me to not ruminate about painful moments from the past. These memories still bare a lot of grief and guilt and I haven't processed them enough to be able to forgive myself.

When I pay attention to my body I notice:

my shins ache when I walk because I've been running too much and not allowing my body to heal.
Tension in my shoulders & upper body in general

When I pay attention to my breath I notice:

my nose is slightly stuffy but I have deep belly breaths!

Discuss how well you did with your practice this week, feelings you had, and obstacles you faced and how you overcame them.

DESIGNER ACTIVITIES

1. Complete the Gratitude Questionnaire.

WHAT THE QUESTIONNAIRE MEASURES

The GQ-6 is a short, self-report measure of the disposition to experience gratitude. Participants answer six items on a 1 to 7 scale (1 = "strongly disagree", 7 = "strongly agree"). Two items are reverse-scored to inhibit response bias. The GQ-6 has good internal reliability, with alphas between .82 and .87, and there is evidence that the GQ-6 is positively related to optimism, life satisfaction, hope, spirituality and religiousness, forgiveness, empathy and prosocial behavior, and negatively related to depression, anxiety, materialism, and envy. The GQ-6 takes less than 5 minutes to complete, but there is no time limit.

The Gratitude Questionnaire-Six Item Form (GQ-6) By Michael E. McCullough, Ph.D., Robert A. Emmons, Ph.D., Jo-Ann Tsang, Ph.D. Using the scale below as a guide, write a number beside each statement to indicate how much you agree with it. 1 = strongly disagree 2 = disagree 3 = slightly disagree 4 = neutral 5 = slightly agree 6 = agree 7 = strongly agree

_____7_____ 1. I have so much in life to be thankful for.

_____5_____ 2. If I had to list everything that I felt grateful for, it would be a very long list.

_____1_____ 3. When I look at the world, I don't see much to be grateful for.*

_____7_____ 4. I am grateful to a wide variety of people.

_____6_____ 5. As I get older I find myself more able to appreciate the people, events, and situations that have been part of my life history.

_____1_____ 6. Long amounts of time can go by before I feel grateful to something or someone.

How to score your questionnaire:

1. Add up your scores for items 1, 2, 4, 5 = 25
2. Reverse your scores for items 3 and 6. That is if you scored a "7" give yourself a "1" if you scored a "6" give yourself a "2" etc. 1: 7; 1: 7 = 14
3. Add the reversed scores for the items 3 and 6 to the total from Step 1. This is your total gratitude questionnaire score. This number should be between 6 and 42. 39

Interpretation:

25th percentile: a score below 35 (bottom quartile)
50th percentile; a score below 38 (bottom half)
75th percentile: a core of 41 (higher than 75%)
Top 13%: a score of 42

* * Items 3 and 6 are reverse-scored.

2. *Thought awareness journal*

   For one week pay attention to your thoughts.

   Keep a journal of positive and negative thinking.

POSITIVE THOUGHTS	NEGATIVE THOUGHTS
I have friends that truly care	I can't provide for Amelia
I am resilient & will get through	Im not strong enough (minded)
Im fit and strong	

3. *Purpose in Life Reminders*

   Find visual reminders of your purpose in life and display them in places where you can see them often such as post its, drawings, and empowering messages.

MY VISUAL LIFE PURPOSE REMINDERS	
REMINDER	WHERE I WILL PLACE IT
Amelia	photos everywhere
liflong learner	books everywhere

4. *Forgiving Yourself*

   Take a photo of yourself, place it on a poster board, purchase "stickies" of hearts or stars and place one each time you forgive yourself for something you said or have done to another person that you regret or have offended.

LIFE BY PERSONAL DESIGN
REFLECTIVE JOURNAL

In this Reflective Journal, record what you learned from this chapter, your "intentions" for change, any barriers you think might interfere with these desired changes and how you will overcome them, and at least *one* strategy that will help you realize your dreams and the life you will love.

_____

_____

_____

_____

_____

_____

_____

_____

_____

_____

_____

_____

_____

_____

_____

_____

_____

_____

_____

_____

_____

_____

READINGS OF INTEREST

Arch, J. J., & Craske, M.G. (2006). Mechanisms of mindfulness: Emotional regulation following a focused breathing induction. *Behavior Research and Therapy 44,* 1849–1958.

Berceli, D., & Napoli, M. (2006). Mindfulness-based trauma-prevention program for social work professionals. *Journal of Complementary Health Practice Review 11:* 153–165.

Carson, S.H., & Langer, E.J. (2006). Mindfulness and self-acceptance. *Journal of Rational-Emotive & Cognitive Behavior Therapy 24,* 29–43.

Dryden, W., & Still, A. (2006). Historical aspects of mindfulness and self-acceptance in psychotherapy. *Journal of Rational-Emotive & Cognitive Behavior Therapy 24(1) spring,* 3–28.

Rothwell, N. (2006). The different facets of mindfulness. *Journal of Rational-emotive and Cognitive-Behavior Therapy 24 (1),* 79–86.

Ryback, D. (2006). Self-determination and the neurology of mindfulness. *Journal of Humanistic Psychology 46 (4) October,* 474–493.

REFERENCES

1. Montepare, Zaitchik, & Albert. (1999). The use of body movement and gestures as cues to emotions in younger and older adults. *Journal of Nonverbal Behavior 23 (2) summer,* 133–152.

2. Schneider, T. R., Lyons, J. B., & Khazon, S. (2013). Emotional intelligence and resilience. *Personality and Individual Differences 55 (8),* 871–876.

3. Sanchez-Alvarez, N. (2016). The relation between emotional intelligence and subjective well being: A meta-analytic investigation. *The Journal of Positive Psychology 11 (3),* 276–285.

4. Napoli, M. (2016). *Tools for mindful living: Practicing the Four Step MAC Guide.* Dubuque, IO: Kendall Hunt.

5. Allen, A. B., & Leary, M. R. (2010). Self-compassion, stress, and coping. *Social Personality and Psychology Compass February 1 4(2),* 107–118.

6. Neff, K. D. (2011). Self-compassion, self-esteem, and well-being. *Journal of Social and Personality Psychology Compass 5(1),* 1–12.

7. Neff, K. D., & Vonk, Roos. (2009). Self-compassion versus global self-esteem: Two different ways of relating to oneself. *Journal of Personality 77 (1),* 23–50.

8. Neff, K. D., Kirkpatrick, K. L., & Rude, S. S. (2007). Self-compassion and adaptive psychological functioning. *Journal of Research in Personality 41,* 139–154.

9. Akin, A. (2010). Self-compassion and loneliness. *International Online Journal of Educational Sciences* 2(3) 702–718.

10. Arimitsu, K. (2016). The effects of a program to enhance self-compassion in Japanese individuals: A randomized controlled pilot study. *Journal of Positive Psychology 11 (6,)* 559–571.

11. Neff, K. D. (2011). Self-compassion, self-esteem, and well-being. *Journal of Social and Personality Psychology Compass 5(1),* 1–12.

12. Allen, A, B., & Leary, M. R. (2010). Self-compassion, stress, and coping. *Journal of Social and Personality Psychology Compass February 1 4(2),* 107–118.

13. Hall, J. H., & Fincham, F. D. (2005). Self forgiveness: The stepchild of forgiveness research. *Journal of Social and Clinical Psychology 24 (50)* 621–637.

14. Hall, J. H., & Fincham, F. D. (2008). The Temporal Course of self forgiveness. *Journal of Social and Clinical Psychology 27(2).* 174–202.

15. McConnell, J. M., Dixon, D. N., & Finch, W. H. (2012). An alternative model of self-forgiveness. *The New School Psychology Bulletin* 9 (2). 35–51.

16. Dickerhoof, R. M. (2007). Expressing optimism and gratitude: a longitudinal investigation of cognitive strategies to increase well being. *Dissertation Abstracts Int. 68:4174B,* 9.

17. Wood, Am M., Joseph, S., & Maltby, J. (2008). Gratitude uniquely predicts satisfaction with life: incremental validity above the domains and facets of the five-factor model. *Personality Individual Differences 45,* 49–54.

18. Chen, L. H., & Kee, Y. H. (2008). Gratitude and adolescent athletes' well being. *Social Indicators Research 89 (2),* 361–373.

19. Froh, J. J. Sefick, Seffick, W. J., & Emmons, R. A. (2008). Counting blessing in early adolescents: an experimental study of gratitude and subjective well being. *Journal of School Psychology 46,* 213–233.

20. Sansone, R. A., & Sansone, L. A. (2010). Gratitude and well being: The benefits of appreciation. *Psychiatry 7(11),* 18–22.

21. Morin, A. (2014). Seven scientifically proven benefits of gratitude that will motivate you to give thanks Year-Round. *Forbes, Entrepreneurs, November 23, 2014 @ 6:12 PM.* http://www.forbes.com/sites/amymorin/2014/11/23/7-scientifically-proven-benefits-of-gratitude-that-will-motivate-you-to-give-thanks-year-round/#567e39126800

22. Abe, J. A. (2016). A longitudinal follow-up study of happiness and meaning making. *Journal of Positive Psychology. 11 (5),* 489–498.

23. Van Tongeren, D. R., Green, J. D., Hook, J. N., & Hulsey, T. L. (2016). Prosociality enhances meaning in life. *Journal of Positive Psychology 11 (3),* 225–236.

24. Hill. P. L., Edmonds, G. W., Peterson, M., Luyckx, L., & Andrews, J. A. (2016). Purpose in life in emerging adulthood: development and validation of a new brief measure. *Journal of Positive Psychology 11 (3),* 237–245.

25. Linley, P. A., & Leontiev, D. (2009). Multiple dimensions of the good life: introducing international and interdisciplinary perspectives. *Journal of Positive Psychology 4 (4),* 257–259.

26. McCullough, M. E., Emmons, R. A., & Tsang, J. (2002). The grateful disposition: A conceptual and empirical topography. *Journal of Personality and Social Psychology, 82,* 112–127.

CHAPTER 2

EATING WITH JOY AND HARMONY

© Antonio Guillem/Shutterstock.com

One cannot think well, love well, sleep well,
if one has not dined well

(Virginia Woolf)

LEARN TO EAT WITH JOY AND HARMONY

- Know your food habits and patterns and how they influence your nutrition and diet
- Be aware of the nutrients that constitute a healthy diet
- Incorporate healthful foods and nutrients into your diet
- Monitor your BMI and, if appropriate, cholesterol levels
- Eat foods that are in harmony with your body
- Look for ways to enjoy and have joy when eating
- Use the Mindful Four Step MAC Guide to eat mindfully

Habits people develop build the foundation and framework for how they conduct their life. A person's eating patterns and the foods they select are examples of life habits learned through exposure and experience. It often does not matter whether a food is "good for you." What matters is how hungry you may be, what you like or even "love" to eat, or what you feel like eating at that moment. It is amazing how difficult it is to change these habits.

© Kzenon/Shutterstock.com

Liking or "loving" a food is central to how people think and feel about their food choices. These choices begin during childhood and are shaped by the food families had access to, their cultural traditions, finances, and what they knew about diet and nutrition. Perhaps certain foods have particular memories for you, both good and not so good! Some foods you eat also have ethnic or cultural origins. As adults your food choices are also influenced by time and resources. Foods may be selected because they are easy to purchase and are accessible such as "fast" foods. Other foods chosen may be "comfort" foods; those foods that make you feel better. These foods may or may not be good for you but they sure do feel "good for you" when you are eating them. What are these foods? Are they pasta, cookies, chocolate, or maybe vegetables, or fruit? How does it feel when you eat them? Do you immediately feel better? This is a singular experience and personal preference.

A recent study of "emerging adults" (ages 18–24) focused on measuring the relative importance of different influences on food choices. Results included a comparison of these influences by gender, adiposity (body mass index or BMI and waist circumference), perceived stress, dieting, and physical activity. The most important influence found was taste. This was followed by convenience, cost, nutritional value, and smell. Those who were heavier selected foods to cope with stress. Conversely, those who had a higher level of physical activity focused more on nutritional value and taste had less importance.[1]

Eating patterns are similarly affected by exposure and experience. Eating patterns also develop from childhood and are usually reinforced during adulthood. These patterns are influenced by how long it takes to feel physically full—about 20 minutes. This is the time needed for the signals between digestion and your brain to let you know you are full. If you eat too fast, that feeling of fullness may occur after you have overeaten.

Digestion, lack of nutritious intake, and weight disorders can all be affected by your eating patterns such as the timing of and distractions while eating. Do you eat slowly or quickly? Do you like to eat more food in the morning or in the evening? Do you snack during the day or are you that person who "raids" the refrigerator during the night? Do you work or drive your car while eating? These patterns become habits and guide your choices of foods and how you eat them.

In addition to the habits and patterns people develop about food and the choices they make, there is new evidence about a physical relationship between the brain and intestines called the "brain-gut interaction." It has been found that the lower intestine, which houses normal flora (bacteria), produces chemicals, which pass through the intestinal wall, and enter the blood circulating to the brain. These chemicals originally created in the intestines causes disturbances in the brain. These disturbances have now been shown to be associated with inflammatory bowel disease, obesity, and eating disorders.[2]

EATING HEALTHFULLY

The food you eat is metabolized in specific ways. Metabolism, the way food is digested and used, is dependent on how foods are organically used by the body systems designed for food consumption, use, and elimination.

You may already be familiar with the different food groups. These are organized as a model called "Choose My Plate" which include the five main food groups (fruits, grains, dairy, protein, and vegetables). These provide the essential nutrients of carbohydrates, fats, proteins, vitamins, minerals, and water. Two links that will give you further information about these food groups,

healthy eating, and recommended daily allowances are https://www.choosemyplate.gov/ and https://health.gov/dietaryguidelines/2015/guidelines/. At these sites you can click on each food group to explore how you can plan for and eat each to ensure you are getting appropriate and adequate nourishment for your body. You can also explore healthy eating patterns. There are also nutrition apps you may find helpful. Some examples can be found in the Readings of Interest section of this chapter.

These foods and the amounts you need to eat are not to be taken lightly. They are what your body needs to function at its optimal level. For children it is an absolute requirement for "normal" growth and development. In addition, the amount of calories (units of food energy) you need will be different or will even change depending on age, body type, activity, and life events (such as pregnancy, chronic conditions, etc.). Another excellent location for information about healthy eating at different ages, nutrients needed, and other aspects of nutrition is www.nutrition.gov.

Vitamins and dietary supplements as well as herbal remedies have become popular ways to also improve nutrition. They are easy to request from providers of health care and are equally as simple to purchase in retail or specialty stores. You can even order them via television, the Internet, or from advertisements in a variety of print publications. There are so many different ones that it can become confusing as to which are appropriate and effective. Further, you must consider which ones you can take given your body type, size and what prescription medication or other supplements you are taking.

"I eat vegetables with lots of antioxidants. That's why I'm still on the first of my nine lives."

Vitamins and minerals are fairly easy to determine as they are contained in the food you eat and recommended dietary allowances (RDA) have been researched for years. You can find more information on vitamins and minerals by linking to https://ods.od.nih.gov/factsheets/list-VitaminsMinerals/

A majority of people in the United States take one or more dietary supplement daily. Dietary supplements are more challenging to make decisions about as they have become popular and accepted in our culture and have become more easily available. Supplements are just that. They are meant to add to your diet and not take the place of what you need to eat healthfully on a daily basis.

Supplements may include vitamins and minerals as discussed previously but they can also be herbals, botanicals, and enzymes. They are usually available as tablets, capsules, powders, drinks, or energy bars. Examples of supplements are Echinacea, St. John's Wort, turmeric, or probiotics (a microbe that stimulates the growth of beneficial microorganisms such as your intestinal flora).

Supplements are not drugs or medicine. The federal agency, the Food and Drug Administration (FDA), provide regulations for dietary supplements. This regulation is not the same as for prescription or over-the-counter medications. Rather, suppliers of dietary supplements must ensure that their products are safe and the label claims are "truthful and not misleading." Taking care when selecting supplements are as important as the time you take when determining your dietary regime. More information about dietary supplements can be found at https://ods.od.nih.gov/factsheets/list-all/ and https://ods.od.nih.gov/factsheets/BotanicalBackground-HealthProfessional/

The Centers for Disease Control and Prevention (CDC) recently reported that 9 out of 10 Americans are receiving a good many of the essential nutrients and vitamins needed such as vitamin D for bone health and iron to avoid anemia (a condition where the blood has less than the normal number of red blood cells thus lessening its capacity to carry sufficient oxygen throughout the body). It is good to know that the status of overall nutrition is adequate, however this is not so for groups such as non-Hispanic blacks who have low levels of vitamin D and Mexican-American and non-Hispanic black women who are at a great risk due to lower levels of iron than non-Hispanic white women.[3]

© szefei/Shutterstock.com

Another important aspect of ensuring healthy eating is the amount of fluid a person drinks each day. Fifty-five to 60% of body weight is water. You can lose quite a bit of water by breathing, sweating, and through elimination. Staying hydrated (having enough fluids in your body daily) is essential no matter what your age, especially if you live in an arid hot climate or if you exercise routinely. It is said that one must drink "8 glasses of water" daily. This is basically true but what does this mean and why do it? Do you only drink water and, if so, what type of water? Can you drink other fluids and which ones should you select? And, finally what is the best way to consume all of this fluid?

The obvious benefits of hydration includes an increase in energy and adequate hydration helps your mood and fosters clarity in thinking. Even the smallest amount of dehydration can slow the body down significantly and cause changes in the cardiovascular, thermoregulatory, metabolic, and central nervous systems. A study of adults 18 to 64 years old revealed that there was a significant association between inadequate hydration, elevated BMI, and obesity even after controlling for age, race/ethnicity, sex, and economics.[4]

The Institute of Medicine (IOM) recommends that an adequate intake (AI) of fluids for men is approximately 15 cups (3.7 liters) of total fluids daily. The AI for women is about 11 cups (2.7 liters) daily. While it has been said that drinking 8 – 8 ounce glasses of water daily (1.9 liters) is a standard, it is clear that this just isn't enough to meet the AI either for men or women.[5] So, more is better!

Daily fluid intake can be from all fluids consumed, which include beverages and foods. Fruits and vegetables contain water and beverages, especially those not caffeinated, are a good source. The temperature of the fluid has some impact. Hot, lukewarm, or cold fluids will have different effects on your body. For example, lukewarm fluid does not have the same drastic impact as hot or cold water because your body does not have to work as hard to respond. Alternating fluid temperatures is recommended. One simple way to determine hydration is to check your urine. If it is pale yellow you are adequately hydrated; however, if the color becomes darker and concentrated, drink more.

The best way to eat healthfully and with joy and harmony is to do just that. Of course this is easy to say but often difficult to do given your lifestyle, financial resources, access to healthy foods, and your responsibilities. But the simple fact is that this is the "truth." Awareness and recognition of what it takes to eat nutritiously is not as demanding as having to deal with being over or underweight or living with chronic conditions resulting from a lifetime of unwise eating patterns and habits.

True!

© Jack Frog/Shutterstock.com

If you have children start them early understanding and becoming familiar and comfortable with eating foods that are "good for them." Interestingly, if your children are eating well, so can you. Become a role model and an exemplar of good eating habits. You can choose to eat well or unfortunately if you don't, the consequences are daunting.

Become a good consumer when selecting your foods at the store. Read the labels on the containers and packages! And, do remember that the label information is based on 2,000 calories a day.

© Yossi Manor/Shutterstock.com

1. Always start at the top of the label. This provides a listing of a single serving size and the total number of servings in that container or package.

2. Check the total calories PER SERVING. Remember the number of servings you consume are the number of calories you actually eat. A general range of calories might be 50 calories per serving, which would be low to 400 calories or more, which would be considered high. The calories from fat is also included. For example, in ONE serving there may be 100 calories from fat for a 200-calorie serving. This means that half of the serving comes from fat.

3. Continuing on, the next part of the label are the nutrients in the food. Based on a 2,000 calorie diet, the American Heart Association (AHA) recommends you consume no more than 11–13 grams of saturated fat, little *trans*-fat, and no more than 1,500 mg. of sodium.

4. Be sure to look at the amount of sugar in the food. Some sugars naturally occur in fruit and milk while other sugars are added to the food. Both are included on the label. There are different types of sugar such as table sugar, also called sucrose. You may also see fructose, which is fruit sugar and lactose, which is the sugar found in milk. There is no recommended daily reference value for sugars however for people with diabetes, or who are obese they must be very aware of how much sugar they consume daily. Having extra sugar not used for energy can convert to triglycerides, a type of fat, which gets stored around your waist, in your hips, and thighs.

5. Also consume sufficient dietary fiber, protein, calcium, iron, and vitamins.

6. The % Daily Value (DV), determined by public health experts, tells you the percentage of each nutrient in a single serving. This is based on the daily recommended amount. For example, if you want to eat less saturated fat or sodium, choose foods with a lower % DV—5 % or less. If you want to consume more fiber or protein, look for a higher % DV such as 20 % or more.[6, 7]

The "obesity epidemic" is a significant health problem. Approximately 40% of adults over 20 years old are considered obese.[8] Adult obesity rates have doubled since 1980, from 15 to 30% and childhood obesity rates have tripled. Being obese results in serious diseases such as diabetes and cardiovascular conditions. As a result, more than one-quarter of US health care costs are now linked to obesity.[9]

© iQoncept/Shutterstock.com

Dieting as a lifestyle pattern to reduce obesity is often temporary and is either not sustained or does not achieve what was intended. The outcome for many who are not successful in eating nutritiously or who do not reach their diet goals is becoming overweight or obese.

One way of determining whether a person is underweight, normal or a healthy weight, overweight, or obese is by using a measure called the body mass index or BMI. This is a calculation of body fat based on an adult man or woman's height and current weight. If the BMI is high it can be an indicator of high body fatness. As an example, a woman is 5' 3" and weighs 158 pounds. When her BMI is calculated it is 28 or "overweight." The range for this category is 25.0 to 29.9. For this person to move to a normal or healthy weight she would need to aim for a weight of 104 to 141 pounds or a BMI of 24.9 or less. This can be helpful for people interested in losing weight as they are given a healthy target to work toward. Do note that BMI is interpreted differently for children and teens due to their continuing developmental height and weight change.[10] If you would like to calculate your BMI go to: http://www.cdc.gov/healthyweight/assessing/bmi/adult_bmi/english_bmi_calculator/bmi_calculator.html

Another important indicator that can be monitored is your total cholesterol levels. This is especially important if you are overweight or obese. Cholesterol is a fat-like substance found in all body cells. It is needed to make vitamins and hormones and to digest food. It is important to realize that your body makes all of the cholesterol it needs so any additional cholesterol in your body is because you have eaten it!

Cholesterol is found in the body as lipoproteins. Their structure is, fat (lipid) on the inside, and it is surrounded by protein on the outside. There are low-density lipoprotein (LDL) or "bad" cholesterol, high-density lipoprotein (HDL) or "good" cholesterol, and triglycerides or the fats carried in the blood converted from excess calories, sugars, or alcohol consumed. A test for cholesterol is usually used to determine risk for heart disease. This a blood test and the results are measured in numbers. Your total cholesterol score is calculated using the following equation: HDL + LDL + 20% of your triglyceride level. Usually each score is looked at individually as well as the total cholesterol level.

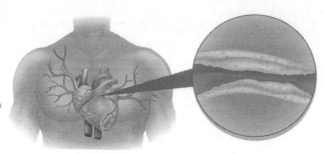

If the LDL cholesterol is high this can mean that "bad" cholesterol has built up on the walls of your arteries lessening the ability of your blood to flow normally. This can cause pressure and lead to high blood pressure (hypertension) and heart disease. A number of 190 or more is considered high and treatment is usually recommended by a healthcare provider along with a modification in diet and exercise. Conversely, if HDL cholesterol is high, this means there is lower risk for heart disease because this cholesterol keeps the bad cholesterol from building up in your arteries. You can see a table that shows recommended cholesterol levels by linking to https://medlineplus.gov/magazine/issues/summer12/articles/summer12pg6-7.html Normally, cholesterol should be measured once every five years for anyone over the age of 20 and more frequently for men over age 35 and women 45 and older unless there is a reason for it to be measured more often.[11, 12]

As discussed, the damage from excess weight is considerable, from dealing with one's body image to chronic disorders such as diabetes and heart disease. Many have gone to more extreme measures to deal with their weight by using laser or surgical procedures as a way to quickly provide an intervention. Often these individuals have tried many other means and found that losing weight by dieting and exercise is not nearly enough. Often, associated illnesses due to being overweight motivated the surgery. You have probably seen or read about many success stories and sadly, failures using this approach. *Bariatrics* has become a specialty in medicine that focuses on the prevention, cause, and treatment of obesity.

On the other side of the "food" coin, are those people who are obsessed with their weight. Their body image may be distorted in that they are a normal weight but they see themselves as overweight or even obese. There is often feelings of shame or anxiety about body size and shape. Many are diagnosed with Anorexia Nervosa (self-starvation), binge eating disorder, or Bulimia Nervosa (binging and purging). These dysfunctional strategies become ways to deal with body image perceptions and are considered eating disorders. The prevalence of these disorders are usually young adults (19, 20, and 25 years old respectively). Binge eating disorders affect 1.2% of the US population (over 3 million people), Anorexia, .6% of the US population, and Bulimia Nervosa, .3%.[13]

Remember that foods entering your mouth are a decision you make on a daily, minute-by-minute basis. Becoming aware of what you eat, how you eat, where you eat, and when you eat is critical to "nourishing yourself." The amount of food you eat impacts your metabolism so that fasting or entering into the world of anorexia or bulimia as a way to control food intake is dangerous. Equally dangerous is the timing of when you eat. Fasting is not particularly kind to your body. Your body craves food on an ongoing basis. Where you eat, such as in front of the television, standing at a counter, or even gobbling food while driving are not the best venues for digestion. Just ask those who face a lifetime of acid reflux (the flow of the stomach's contents back up into the esophagus) now commonly known as gastroesophageal reflux disease (GERD). So simply paying attention to your particular "brand" of nutrition is a wonderful life goal.

DIETS, DIETS, AND MORE DIETS

Dieting has become a way of life for many who are or who perceive themselves as "not at that right weight." These range from simple diets constructed by one's own desires and imagination to those diets purchased either by buying a book, going to classes and seminars, purchasing specific food provided under the diet's requirements, and/or seeing a healthcare provider. There are so many opportunities to try a different diet that for some it seems overwhelming to even begin. Others take a buffet approach and try some or many different diets. The bottom line on dieting is that no matter what approach you take you must always be aware that your body must be nourished with appropriate combinations of essential nutrients such as protein, carbohydrates, and fats. The most important part of dieting is to not do it alone. Consult a healthcare provider about what type of diet may work best for you particularly if you have a chronic illness or condition.

So does this Flamingo diet have any side effects?

Cartoonstock.com

With so many diets available, such as gluten free, vegan, and ketogenic to those diets that supply their own food, it is not possible to provide a concise list in this chapter. Feel free to link to http://www.diet.com/info/encyclopedia-of-diets/; a site where the American Dietetic Association provides a considerable range of diets in alphabetical order. You can search for a specific diet or browse. For each you will find its definition, origin, description, function, benefits, precautions, risks, research and general acceptance, and resources.[14]

As you begin to think more about your diet, the first step you can take is to make the decision that eating healthfully can and should be an important part of your lifestyle. Next, practice good eating behaviors, explore new ways of preparing your food, and what foods and strategies will work for you so you can make good choices. Finally, integrate foods you like and love that are in harmony with your body's health and lifestyle. This approach can lead you to a life of enjoying the food you eat and ensuring that you are satisfying your body's needs and personal palate (appreciation for taste and flavor).

MINDFUL EATING

Mindfulness has given me the gift of staying in the moment until I am ready for the next bite.

Elizabeth Marques

Many of us seem to be so busy that even eating is done quickly, without thought, and is soon forgotten. As discussed earlier, this approach to eating can lead to issues and problems that not only affect a person's weight but can also lead to challenging and serious diseases and disorders. Eating more carefully and thoughtfully has been shown to promote better choices and decisions. This approach is called "mindful eating." It is based on concept of mindfulness learned in chapter 1. That is, being fully aware of what is happening within and around you at that moment.

Eat mindfully by focusing your entire mind-body on the smell, taste, sight, and texture of the food as there is nothing in the world but the food and you.

Karen R. Koenig

A mindful eating technique treatment (randomized control study) was recently conducted. It included 150 binge eaters. It compared a mindfulness-based therapy to a standard psychoeducational treatment. There was also a control group. Both treatments resulted in decreasing binging and lessening depression; however the mindfulness-based therapy appeared to help participants better enjoy their food, recognize the difference between emotional and physical hunger, and struggle less with controlling their eating by becoming aware that there is a "moment of choice" between the urge to eat and eating. Further, it was found that those who also meditated received more payoff from the treatment.[15]

If you are not already eating mindfully, here are some strategies that can help you start. Mindful eating can make the difference between "just eating" and eating healthfully!

1. Before preparing to eat, take a breath. Ask yourself, "Am I really hungry?" Try some other activity first such as reading or taking a short walk to see if your hunger is emotional or physical.

2. Select one meal during the week to begin eating mindfully. You can start by just eating more slowly and paying attention to what you are eating (avoid mindless eating). Take small bites, enjoy them, and chew your food well.

3. Be sure you are eating your meal at a table used for dining. Sit in a chair. Avoid eating where you will be reclining or casually relaxing on a sofa.

4. When you are more comfortable eating slowly, set a timer for 20 minutes and take that full amount of time to eat a normal-sized meal.

5. Try using different eating strategies to slow you down such as eating with your non-dominant hand or use chopsticks.

6. Pay attention to portion sizes. Here is a handy guide you can use to judge appropriate portion size. http://www.webmd.com/diet/printable/portion-control-size-guide. You also don't need to be a member of the "clean plate club."

7. Experiment with eating silently. Make eating a special inner experience. Think about what it took to make the meal, and the great benefits you will have by eating joyously and in harmony with your body.[16]

MINDFULNESS PRACTICE
USING THE MINDFUL MAC GUIDE

The 4 Step MAC Guide will help you practice mindfulness.

1. Empathically **acknowledge** an experience you had this week without internal or external filters
2. Intentionally pay **attention** to your senses, thoughts, emotions, and instincts regarding this experience
3. **Accept** the experience without judgment or expectations
4. **Choose** to respond versus reacting to the experience

Discuss how well you did with your practice this week, feelings you had, obstacles you faced and how you overcame them.

_____

_____

_____

_____

_____

_____

_____

_____

_____

_____

_____

_____

_____

_____

_____

_____

_____

_____

_____

DESIGNER ACTIVITIES

Please answer the following:

1. What foods do you like the most? Which do you like the least?

   fresh fruit and vegtables, salmon, eastern european cuisine the most. Not a huge fan of spicy too painful to eat, not enjoyable

2. What foods have memories for you?

   Pelmeni, borsht, kvass, Ukrainian dishes grew up eating them

3. What snacks do you eat daily? When do you eat those snacks? Are they nutritious snacks or ones that have "empty" calories?

   I dont like to keep unhealthy snacks around because I'll want to eat them. Usually nuts/seeds or fruit. Pita chips w/hummus or if I want something sweet sometime cereal w/soy milk

4. Look at yourself in the mirror. Decide. From your perspective, are you overweight, underweight, or just at the right weight? As a matter of reference look at what weight is considered appropriate for your height and body type. What is your BMI? What did you find out?

   I think I'm at just the right weight. The BMI calculator states that I'm at a normal weight: 22 BMI (5'3" 124 pounds) (18.5-24.9 normal) I would ideally like to be at 20 BMI (118/119 lbs)

5. Start a diary or list of what you eat each day. Be honest. Identify everything that enters your mouth. Do this for a week and then evaluate if you are eating all food groups and recommended allowances. Are there any goals you need to set to make changes in your diet?

Coffee
tofu scramble
Beyond beef burger / Dr. Pepper / fries
Green tea / rodeios tea

6. If you have been on a diet recently, identify the diet you were on. Was the diet successful or not successful? Explain.

I decided to become vegetarian (about a year) then transitioned to veganism for half a year. My body is in the best shape its been in ever. I decided to adopt a majority plant based diet now but will occasionally still. eat fish

7. If you are thinking about a particular diet, research it in the *Encyclopedia of Diets* and describe what you found about the diet in terms of whether it is the right one for you.

The reason why I had to transition away from a solely vegan diet is because I was becoming malnourished and anemic. It was not right for me, but it taught me a lot

8. If you are on a diet now, assess whether the diet is providing you with adequate nutrition. If not, set goals if you believe you need to make changes.

my diet now consists of only things that are beneficial to me.

9. Purchase a small notebook and write down how much you drink each day. Do it in estimated ounces. Add it up daily and then look at how much you have had to drink. Do this for a week. If you are not getting enough to drink, add different types of fluids into your daily pattern and find times you would not normally take something to drink and do it.

© artpritsadee/
Shutterstock.com

I have a 32oz hydro flask. I know if I can empty two full flasks in one day then I've had the proper amount of fluids

10. Look at the vitamins and/or supplements you are taking. Write a short description of each by doing research on them. Link them to the food you eat and set goals if you believe a change is needed. You may also want to talk with a healthcare provider about what you are taking and the impact it may have on any prescription medications you are taking.

11. Think about the last time you went to a restaurant. What foods did you select and eat. Were they nutritious? If not, what foods might you have eaten that would have been better nourishment for your body?

© Monkey Business
Images/Shutterstock.com

I typically always pick the healthiest options available because they seem the most appetizing

LIFE BY PERSONAL DESIGN
REFLECTIVE JOURNAL

In this Reflective Journal, record what you learned from this chapter, your "intentions" for change, any barriers you think might interfere with these desired changes, and how you will overcome them, and at least *one* strategy that will help you realize your dreams and the life you will love.

READINGS OF INTEREST

There are many resources in the areas of nutrition, diets, healthy eating, and eating disorders. Here are several for you to explore.

American Dietetic Association

http://www.eatright.org/

Staying away from fad diets. http://www.eatright.org/resource/health/weight-loss/
  fad-diets/staying-away-from-fad-diets

Count your Calories for a Healthier Lifestyle

https://www.caloriecount.com/

Harvard T. H. Chan School of Public Health

The Nutrition Source. https://www.hsph.harvard.edu/nutritionsource/

Health.Gov

Dietary Guidelines. https://health.gov/DietaryGuidelines/

Mayo Clinic

Healthy Lifestyle: Weight Loss. http://www.mayoclinic.org/healthy-lifestyle/weight-loss/
  in-depth/weight-loss/art-20048466?p=1

Healthy Lifestyle: Organic foods: Are they safer? More nutritious? http://www.mayoclinic
  .org/healthy-lifestyle/nutrition-and-healthy-eating/in-depth/organic-food/art-20043880

**National Association of Anorexia Nervosa and Associated Disorders—
  Eating Disorders**

http://www.anad.org/get-information/about-eating-disorders/

National Center for Complementary and Integrative Health

The Use of Complementary and Alternative Medicine in the United States. https://nccih.
  nih.gov/research/statistics/2007/camsurvey_fs1.htm

National Heart, Lung, and Blood Institute

Aim for a healthy weight. http://www.nhlbi.nih.gov/health/educational/lose_wt/index.htm

National Institutes of Mental Health—Eating Disorders

https://www.nimh.nih.gov/health/topics/eating-disorders/index.shtml

O'Keefe, J.H. (2008). Nutrition 101: Physicians can no longer ignore the healing power
  of diet and nutritional supplements. *Expert Review of Cardiovascular Therapy, 6*(5),
  593–596.

President's Council on Fitness, Sports, & Nutrition

http://www.fitness.gov/eat-healthy/useful-resources/

Sadovsky, R., Collins, N., Tighe, A. P., Brunton, S. A., & Safeer, R. (2008). Patient use of dietary supplements: A clinician's perspective. *Current Medical Research and Opinion, 24*(4), 1209–1216.

Schmidt, L., & Napoli, M. (2015). *Sustainable living and mindful eating.* Dubuque, IA: Kendall Hunt Publishing Company.

Sharpe, P. A., Blanck, H. M., Williams, J. E., Ainsworth, B. E., & Conway, J. M. (2007). Use of complementary and alternative medicine for weight control in the United States. *Journal of Alternative and Complementary Medicine, 13*(2), 217–222.

The 5 Best Nutrition Apps, According to RDs, Health, http://www.health.com/nutrition/best-nutrition-apps

Tufts Health & Nutrition Letter

Healthy Eating. http://www.nutritionletter.tufts.edu/topics/healthy-eating.html

Vitamins and Supplements. http://www.nutritionletter.tufts.edu/topics/vitamins-supplements.html

US Department of Agriculture (USDA)

Dietary Assessment. https://www.nal.usda.gov/fnic/individual-dietary-assessment

Dietary Guidance. https://www.nal.usda.gov/fnic/dietary-guidance-0

Dietary Interactive Tools. https://www.nal.usda.gov/fnic/interactive-tools

Eating Disorders. https://www.nal.usda.gov/fnic/disordered-eating

REFERENCES

1. Hebden, L., Chan, H. N., Louie, J.C., Rangan, A., & Allman-Farinell, M. (2015). You are what you choose to eat: Factors influencing young adults' food selection behaviour. *Journal of Human Nutrition & Dietetics, 28*(4), 401–408.

2. Mayer, E. A. (2011). Gut feelings: The emerging biology of gut-brain communication. *Nature Reviews Neuroscience, 12*(8), 453–466.

3. Centers for Disease Control and Prevention. CDC's Second Nutrition Report: Infographic 2012 Findings from the Second Nutrition Report. http://www.cdc.gov/nutritionreport/infographic.html

4. Chang, R., Ravi, N., Plegue, M. A., Sonnevile, K. R., & Davis, M. M. (2016). Inadequate hydration, BMI, and obesity among US adults: NHANES 2009–2012. *Annals of Family Medicine, 14*(4): 320–324.

5. The National Academies of Sciences, Engineering, Medicine. Institute of Medicine Dietary Reference Intake Tables and Application (2010). Electrolyte and Water Summary.

6. American Heart Association. Understanding Food Nutrition Labels. http://www.heart.org/HEARTORG/HealthyLiving/HealthyEating/Nutrition/Understanding-Food-Nutrition-Labels_UCM_300132_Article.jsp#.V-_pFIWcHIU

7. US Food and Drug Administration. (2016). Food Labels. http://www.fda.gov/Food/GuidanceRegulation/GuidanceDocumentsRegulatoryInformation/LabelingNutrition/ucm385663.htm http://www.fda.gov/Food/IngredientsPackagingLabeling/LabelingNutrition/ucm274593.htm#overview

8. Centers for Disease Control & Prevention (CDC). (2015). Overweight and Obesity. Data and Statistics http://www.cdc.gov/nccdphp/dnpa/obesity/trend/index.htm

9. Trust for America's Health. (2016). TFAH Issues. Obesity http://healthyamericans.org/obesity/

10. Centers for Disease Control & Prevention (CDC). (2015). Healthy Weight. About Adult BMI. http://www.cdc.gov/healthyweight/assessing/bmi/adult_bmi/index.html

11. National Heart, Lung, & Blood Institute. What is Cholesterol? http://www.nhlbi.nih.gov/health/health-topics/topics/hbc/

12. NIH Medline Plus. (2012). Cholesterol Levels: What You Need to Know. Measuring Cholesterol Levels. https://medlineplus.gov/magazine/issues/summer12/articles/summer12pg6-7.html

13. National Institute of Mental Health. Eating Disorders Among Adults. https://www.nimh.nih.gov/health/statistics/prevalence/eating-disorders-among-adults-anorexia-nervosa.shtml https://www.nimh.nih.gov/health/statistics/prevalence/eating-disorders-among-adults-bulimia-nervosa.shtml https://www.nimh.nih.gov/health/statistics/prevalence/eating-disorders-among-adults-binge-eating-disorder.shtml

14. American Dietetic Association. Diets A-Z. http://www.diet.com/info/

15. Kristeller, J. L., & Wolever, R. Q. (2011). Mindfulness-based eating awareness training for treating binge eating disorder: The conceptual foundation, *Eating Disorders. 19*(1), 49–61.

16. Sources include the following: The Center for Mindful Eating http://www.thecenterformindfuleating.org/, Am I Hungry http://amihungry.com/what-is-mindful-eating/, and Mindful Eating http://www.health.harvard.edu/staying-healthy/mindful-eating

CHAPTER 3

MAXIMIZING YOUR BODY'S VITALITY

© soiarseven/Shutterstock.com

Fear less, hope more, eat less, chew more; whine
less, breathe more; talk less, say more; love
more, and all good things will be yours.

(Swedish Proverb)

LEARN TO MAXIMIZE YOUR BODY'S VITALITY

- Consider the influence of your body image on your life
- Identify your body type
- Understand the importance of mobility
- Pursue your favorite recreation and play to increase your activity level
- Integrate regular physical activity into your daily life
- Use the Mindful Four Step MAC Guide to maximize your body's vitality

There are mirrors everywhere! Some mirrors reflect what you actually look like to yourself and to others. These mirrors reveal what you "see" as your reflected body image. The mirror may show a true reality or what you perceive your reality to be, the way you see yourself. Sometimes you are perfectly happy with your image and other times you wish it were different. Different may be your longing to be shorter or taller, thinner or fatter, prettier or even more confident in the way you handle your life affairs.

© stefanolunardi/Shutterstock.com

BODY IMAGE AND TYPES

Body image is related to developmental messages and the creation of your self-esteem. But no matter how you perceive yourself, whether it reflects reality or not, the image you have affects the actions and decisions you make in your everyday life. You think about your body image with every step you take, whether it be a conscious or subconscious act. Your image even shadows the life decisions you make, such as what career you are capable of, whom you may have relationships with, even down to the clothes you buy, the car you select, the house you live in, and the food you buy.

You may wonder what influences your body image. For one, the media, both written and broadcast, play a large role. The next time you are at the food market or drugstore, go to the magazine shelf. Scan the magazines that relate to fashion, beauty, or even family lifestyle. What you will see are images of very attractive, thin, and fit men and women. Even the men and women who are older reflect this same image. Certainly "models" have always had the stereotype of being extremely thin, often emaciated. Thankfully, in the recent past and currently, the fashion industry is beginning to be more aware that "average weight" people cannot and are not able to maintain such a slim body structure. From a business and marketing perspective we are now starting to see models whose attributes are "curvier."

Body image also emanates from the messages you received as a child and the significant others you lived with. If fitness and physical activity were thought to be important and a conscious part of your growing up, you will likely maintain that as an adult and see yourself as someone who is active and who wants to be fit. As an adult, if your partner or friends are involved in exercise or sports activities, you will likely want to participate, even if your goal is more social than physical.

Will a positive body image make a difference? Will you be more happy and adjusted, and find more joy in your life? It won't hurt. However, remember your body image must be realistic. You need to work with what you have. Try not to compare yourself with others and stop those negative thoughts if you don't match up. Rather celebrate and nurture what you have. Find the joy in what you can do and invest in yourself.

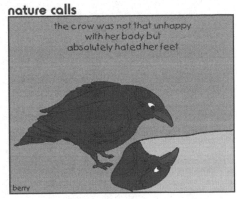

nature calls

the crow was not that unhappy with her body but absolutely hated her feet

berry

Cartoonstock.com

There are certain body types that have been identified as body "models" or soma types. Developed originally by Sheldon in the early 1940s as a way of classifying physiology with a person's temperament, today they are one of the ways used to understand different body structures and to determine your body type.[1]

Are you an Ectomorph? Ectomorphs have a thin build with little muscle and fat. They have difficulty gaining weight. This body type is not able to manage great amounts of athletic training. Ectomorphs have a higher metabolism to keeps fat levels in check.

Are you a Mesomorph? Mesomorphs are very athletic with a muscular frame that has relatively low amounts of body fat. Mesomorphs do not have trouble losing fat and easily gain muscle. They have a higher metabolism to keep fat levels in check.

Are you an Endomorph? Endomorphs have a large rounder body with high levels of fat and more muscle density. Endomorphs have trouble losing weight but an easier time gaining muscle as well as fat.

What does body type have to do with your vitality? It helps you think through the kinds of activities that may fit your body type, allowing you to design a specific and active lifestyle that aligns with proper and routine physical fitness.

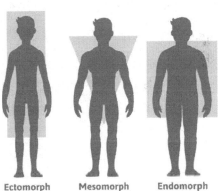

Ectomorph   Mesomorph   Endomorph

© *Sudowoodo/Shutterstock.com*

IMPORTANCE OF MOBILITY

You are designed for motion and activity. This is why your body has the number of bones (approximately 206) and muscles (640 muscles or 320 pairs), as well as having joints and tendons. Regular and appropriate physical activity contribute to keeping these properly positioned and moving to promote your health and well-being. Immobility, on the other hand, has a negative effect. Not adequately moving your muscles and joints can literally cause them to stiffen in as quickly as 24 hours. Long periods of joint immobility may also influence your muscles and tendons and cause them to become rigid and inflexible. Immobility can also affect other parts of your body such as your gastrointestinal system causing heartburn, indigestion, and constipation. Prolonged immobility, such as sitting at a desk for extended periods of time or on an extremely long airplane trip can lead to the development of a blood clot in a deep vein called "deep vein thrombosis" or DVT. This condition can be very serious. It is recommended that you stand and move one to two minutes for every 20 to 30 minutes of sitting. If you are on an airplane, regular trips to the bathroom is advised as well as exercising your calf muscles while sitting.[2, 3]

Cartoonstock.com

Another important factor influencing mobility is body alignment. Alignment is the optimal placement of your body parts so that your bones and muscles are used efficiently. When your body is aligned properly you can achieve a good posture. Your mobility, when you walk, climb stairs, sit in front of a computer, or drive a car, as examples, happens through constriction of muscles which move your bones with the help of the connective tissue that joins the two together. For example, if you constrict the muscle on your upper arm, it moves your forearm by pulling on the tendon that goes across the elbow. This action is considered the "mechanics" of how your body works.

Possessing good posture and body mechanics helps reduce possible injuries such as low back or shoulder pain or strain particularly when you are using a computer for long periods of time, bending down, or lifting something. Another way of preventing injuries is through ergonomics, which is, designing the workplace to fit the person. In other words, in some work settings you will see people sitting in specially designed ergonomically fitted chairs or using "standing desks."

Whether you are in a workplace ergonomically designed or not, here are some handy tips to ensure you maintain a good posture and use proper body mechanics.[4, 5]

When Sitting in a Chair	Your buttocks should be all the way to the back of the chair, your back should be straight and your shoulders back. Bend your knees so they are at right angles. They should be at the same height or slightly lower than your hips. Your feet should be flat on the floor.
When Lifting	Check the load you are lifting. Get help if it is ⅓ to ½ your body weight. Use your stronger leg muscles for lifting. Bend your knees and hips keeping your back straight. Lower your body down to meet the object you are trying to pick up. Never stoop or bend at the waist with your legs straight. Lift the object straight up in one smooth motion using your leg muscles to return to an upright position.
When Reaching for an Object	Before moving an object make sure it is not too large or heavy. Stand directly in front of the object making sure you are close to it. Avoid twisting or stretching. Use a stool or ladder for high objects but check the stool or ladder first to make sure it is stable and will support you.

How is your body's alignment, posture, and do you use good body mechanics? Do you slump when you are standing or when you are seated in a chair? Do you bend your knees when you pick something up from the floor? Do you make sure you don't sit for long periods of time without getting up, walking, and stretching your body?

Ambulation, or the ability to walk around, is essential to daily living as it improves circulation and muscle tone (having the right amount of "tension" inside muscles when at rest and the ability to contract muscles on command), preserves lung tissue and airway function, and safeguards muscle and joint mobility.

The way a person walks or runs is called gait. The gait cycle is composed of two actions; the stance and swing. Stance (62% of the cycle) is when the foot is in contact with the ground. Swing (38% of the cycle) is when the foot is in the air.[6] People begin to walk independently at approximately 11 months old. By the time they are adults, they are walking about 3.1 miles per hour (mph). This depends however on height, weight, age, fitness level, effort, culture, the ground, surface, and load.[7] Walking differs from running. During walking, one leg is always in contact with the ground, while the other is swinging. When running, there is typically a time where both feet are off the ground at the same time.[8]

© ChameleonsEye/Shutterstock.com

PHYSICAL FITNESS AND PHYSICAL LITERACY

There are several dimensions of physical fitness and physical literacy to explore. To begin the discussion, if you were to ask people about their physical fitness they would likely describe their activity level based on their perspective and feelings about exercise, experiences with exercise, and probably their most recent attempts at exercise. For some, the answer would be easy because they exercise routinely, but for others the answer might be more difficult. What about you? What would be your answer?

Physical fitness is the state of health and well-being comprised of physical exercise, physical activity such as playing sports, proper nutrition, and adequate rest. The goal of specific physical fitness activities is to balance five key components that signify physical fitness health.

© El Nariz/Shutterstock.com

1. Aerobic exercise or cardiac or endurance exercise. Aerobic exercises include walking, jogging, biking, swimming, dancing, or performing some active household chores.

   These cause you to breathe faster and more deeply. This maximizes the amount of oxygen in your blood making your heart, lungs, and blood vessels more efficient and better able to transport oxygen throughout your body.

2. Strength training or muscular fitness. This training helps increase bone strength, muscle fitness, and reduces body fat. Hand-held weights, resistance bands, pushups, abdominal crunches, leg squats or resistance machines and free weights can be used for strength training.

3. **Core exercises.** These exercises focus on building the muscles in your abdomen, lower back, and pelvis. Any exercise is considered core if you are using the trunk of your body without support. Abdominal crunches or fitness balls are often used as core exercises.

4. **Balance training.** This training is particularly effective for older adults, and is also beneficial for any one as it helps stabilize core muscles. For example, standing on one leg for increasing periods of time will improve balance. It has also been found that tai chi (gentle slow exercise and stretching accompanied by deep breathing) can also promote balance.

5. **Stretching for flexibility.** Stretching improves the range of motion of joints, promotes better posture, and can help relieve stress. Warm-ups are important before stretching exercises (low intensity walking for 5–10 minutes). Stretching can and should be included after exercise when muscles are warm and are more receptive to stretching. If you don't exercise regularly, to maintain flexibility, consider stretching routinely particularly when you have been sitting at a computer for long periods of time. Yoga is also an excellent option to promote flexibility.[9]

It has been consistently shown that physical fitness can improve health and well-being even for those who have chronic diseases and disabilities. Physical activity can lower the risk of early death, cardiovascular conditions and diseases, Type 2 diabetes, and even depression. For children and adolescents it improves bone health, decreases body fat, and improves cardio-respiratory and muscular fitness. For the elderly, physical activity can prevent bone loss, reduce the risk of fractures from falling, and other diseases associated with aging. Interestingly, being physically active has such power that even a small increase in activity can yield health benefits.[10]

To achieve physical fitness, activity and exercise must be done regularly. For this to occur, it is essential that people have "physical literacy." "Physical literacy is the motivation, confidence, physical competence, knowledge, and understanding to value and take responsibility for engagement in physical activities for life."[11] The intention "for life" is an important element in this definition.

In a recent qualitative review of literature the importance of one aspect of physical literacy, health-related fitness knowledge (HRFK), and its influence on increasing physical activity (PA) and physical fitness (PF) was explored. The findings indicated that HRFK is low among elementary-aged through college-aged students; HRFK has successfully predicted PA and PF levels, though research is limited; and educational interventions such as conceptual physical education (CPE) or personal fitness classes has shown a longitudinal increase in the levels of PA and PF.[12]

Ways to increase physical literacy is very helpful to know given the alarming US statistics regarding physical activity.[13]

- About 1 in 5 (21%) adults meet the 2008 Physical Activity Guidelines for aerobic and muscle-strengthening activity
- 49% of adults 18 years of age and over meet the Physical Activity Guidelines for aerobic physical activity

- Less than 3 in 10 high school students get at least 60 minutes of physical activity daily
- 18 year olds spend on average 7.5 hours a day watching TV, working on computers, playing video games, and talking on their cell phones.[14]

What can be done to improve these statistics and improve physical literacy? Let's look at the use of recreation and play as one possible strategy.

RECREATION AND PLAY

© Dudarev Mikhail/
Shutterstock.com

Recreation is defined as "an activity that people engage in during their free time that people enjoy, and that people recognize as having socially redeeming values." This is different than leisure. Recreation usually contributes to society in acceptable ways. Physical recreation includes sports, games, travel, reading, arts and crafts, and dance. The goal of recreation is to help balance lives, and provide a refreshing break from work and household chores.

Play, in contrast, while still seen as recreation is less organized, always fun, is inner motivated, and actively engaging. Play because of its spontaneity is joyful and can be stress reducing. When people think of play they often believe it is only for children. More recently, adults have found play to be equally joyful, pleasurable, and stress reducing.[15]

Play starts at birth when babies begin to explore. They touch and hold, reach and shake, and grab and taste. They discover the world with their limbs and all of their senses. These activities, considered play, help babies make new observations and choices, and expand their imaginations and creativity.

Through play, children develop social skills, learn to cooperate, and work in groups. They explore, invent, and create. They begin to understand their emotions and improve their physical capacities and abilities. As children grow they acquire strength and new physical skills by climbing, running, hopping, skipping, and jumping. To reach a healthy weight, children need 60 minutes of play with moderate to vigorous activity daily. Adolescents use play to experiment and test possibilities. Through organized sports and physical recreation, children and adolescents develop communication and negotiation skills, and leadership which helps build confidence. Sports, defined as "physical activity that contributes to physical fitness, mental well-being, and social interaction," helps them enjoy a sense of community and belonging, friendship, fair play, teamwork, self-discipline, trust, respect for others, and learn coping skills.[16]

Because sports are seen as a universal language and recreation and play are so powerful in educating and developing, they help bridge divides among people and promote core values, release tension and lessen cultural differences and political agendas. A UNICEF international policy initiative uses sports and physical activity as part of their agenda for development, communication, and social mobilization of countries with a particular emphasis on young people.[16]

© stockphoto-graf/
Shutterstock.com

On average, Americans spend approximately 4.5 to 5 hours in recreation/leisure activities or at play daily.[17] Understanding the importance of recreation and play, why not encourage and use these hours for increased physical activity. Currently, recreational fitness and adult play are emerging as strategies to increase physical activity and fitness. It makes sense, it is healthy, and it is also fun!

PHYSICAL FITNESS AND EXERCISE

The earlier question raised, "what can be done to improve the alarming physical fitness statistics in the United States and improve physical literacy" can also be approached through exercise. The obvious benefits of exercise are:

- maintaining joint mobility
- preventing muscle weakness
- stimulating circulation to prevent DVT formation
- improving coordination
- building and maintaining muscle strength

So, if it is a fact that exercise improves health and well-being, what factors are barriers for people to not exercise? There are two categories of non-exercise behaviors: sedentary, which is sitting, lying down, and expending minimal energy and light-intensity and low-energy activities, which are standing, self-care activities, and slow walking.[18]

Other possible barriers that contribute to non-exercise or light-intensity activity include:

- Lack of time
- Low motivation
- Perception that a great amount of energy is needed
- Overweight or obesity
- Perception of poor health
- Transportation needed to exercise facilities
- Cost of exercise
- Advancing age
- Low income
- Being disabled[19]

Just as with weight, exercise and active life styles require thought, the ability to overcome barriers, and then taking action. If you are already exercising, is it the "right" exercise for you? Is it adding to the strength of your body or is it just a ritual that has become habit forming? Remember that the endorphins secreted during exercise gives you a "personal high," but may not be adding to the strength quotient you would like to achieve. If you are not exercising at all, what is keeping you from adding this to your "personal life design?"

Determining the best way to exercise may take some research and perhaps consultation. For some, exercising at home with a prescribed routine works well. Others seek personal trainers who provide more discipline and focused activity. Even others find going to a gym the best way to maximize their body's vitality and also take care of their social needs. And, others participate in sports or recreational activities to increase their physical activity. Whatever it is, your body needs routine physical activity.

© nd3000/Shutterstock.com

If you have not exercised or haven't for some time and/or you have health issues, it is important to talk with your healthcare provider before starting a new personal physical fitness program. Starting a new program can be exhilarating and also overwhelming at the same time. It is helpful to plan and pace yourself so your program becomes an integral part of your life pattern. Take the time you need, be patient, and give exercise a chance. Also, do not over-exercise and take care that you do not become a "weekend warrior" where you save all of your physical activity and exercise for Saturday and Sunday. Finally, allow yourself to rejoice in the experience of improved fitness and feeling better. Remember you don't need to join a gym. You can look for ways in your daily pattern of living to increase your heart rate and deep breathing.

When designing your program, consider your fitness goals. Examine your desires, set your goals, identify potential barriers, and find ways you can overcome these barriers. You can use the format below to get started.

SETTING YOUR FITNESS GOALS[20]

List two long-term fitness goals. Be specific, such as "I want to exercise 30 minutes five times a week."

   1.

   2.

List at least two short-term goals for each long-term goal. For example, "By March 1, I will exercise 20 minutes three times a week."

   1.

   2.

What do you see as barriers to exercising? Check all that apply.

No time		Too tired		Inconvenient	
Can't find time		Rather not be sore		Uncomfortable	
Easily discouraged		Family obligations		Apprehensive	
Lack of discipline		Work obligations		Don't see value	
Failed in the past		Don't want to sweat		Boring	

Other: _____

Of the barriers checked, pick your two greatest barriers. Write a possible solution for the barrier.

1. _____ Barrier

Solution:

2. _____ Barrier

Solution:

When developing the plan itself, be aware that you want to balance the five key components that signify fitness health: aerobic exercise, strength training, core exercises, balance training, and stretching.

Overall, recommendations based on the *Physical Activity Guidelines for Americans* in 2008 indicate that your daily life activities—doing active chores around the house, yard work, walking the dog—will also count.

Here are some specific guidelines.[21, 22, 23, 24]

AEROBIC EXERCISE

Adults should get at least 150 minutes of moderate-intensity aerobic or 75 minutes of vigorous activity per week. This can be walking, jogging, swimming, bicycling, or even dancing. One continuous session and multiple shorter sessions (of at least 10 minutes) are both acceptable to reach these daily exercise goals. Gradual progression of exercise time and its frequency and intensity is advised for best adherence and least risk for injury.

Cartoonstock.com

"OK, now let's start focusing on the left arm."

STRENGTH TRAINING

For adults, strength training should occur at least two to three days a week with two to four sets of each exercise; 8–12 repetitions to help improve strength and power and/or 15–20 to improve muscle endurance. For middle age or older adults, 10–15 repetitions will improve strength. Adults should wait at least 48 hours between strength training sessions.

BALANCE TRAINING

For adults, two to three days, 20–30 minutes per week for balance training. This can include exercises using motor skills, agility, coordination, and gait.

STRETCHING

Adults should perform stretching exercises at least two or three days each week to improve their range of motion. Each stretch should be repeated two to four times, and held 10–30 seconds to the point of tightness or slight discomfort. The muscles should be warm to increase flexibility. Keep the stretches gentle. Breathe freely during each stretch. The breath should not be held. Don't bounce or hold a painful stretch. Expect to feel tension during stretching. If pain is felt, stop!

Mind-body practices that focus on movement are also helpful. They emphasize the interaction between the brain, mind, body, and behavior. The intent is to use the mind and the body to affect physical functioning to promote health. In a recent study, it was shown that 10.1% of US adults had used yoga, tai chi, or qui gong. Yoga has grown with almost twice as many adults practicing yoga in 2012 as in 2002.[25]

© wavebreakmedia/Shutterstock.com

The mind-body practices focusing on movement are as follows:

TYPE OF MOVEMENT THERAPY	DESCRIPTION
Yoga	Combines physical postures, breathing techniques, and meditation or relaxation. There are numerous schools of yoga. Hatha yoga, the most commonly practiced in the United States and Europe, emphasizes postures *(asanas)* and breathing exercises *(pranayama)*. See chapter 4 for more information about Yoga.
Pilates	Uses physical exercise to strengthen and build control of muscles, especially those used for posture. Awareness of breathing and precise control of movements are essential.
Qi Gong	Involves slow fluid movements, deep breathing, and meditative state of mind. Qi gong may ease fibromyalgia pain, reduce chronic neck pain, and improve general quality of life.
Tai Chi	Involves certain postures and gentle movements with mental focus, breathing, and relaxation. In contrast to qi gong, tai chi movements, if practiced quickly, can be a form of combat or self-defense. Tai chi may help to improve balance and stability in older people and those with Parkinson's disease. It may also reduce back pain, improve reasoning ability in older people, and promote quality of life and mood in people with heart failure and cancer.

As you work on your physical fitness plan, pay special attention to issues and concerns should you decide to purchase exercise equipment. Be skeptical about testimonials, models, or celebrity endorsements. What works for one person may not work for another. Ignore claims that the equipment can provide long lasting, easy, "no sweat" results. Also, that it will "burn a spare tire" or "melt fat from your hips." You must regularly exercise your whole body to get the needed benefits. Also, be sure what you are buying. Ask if you can take a "test drive" to see if it is the right fit for you. Read reviews, shop around for the best price and real cost, look at the small print, get warranties and return policies, and ask if there is technical and customer support.[26]

You may also choose to use assistive devices such as pedometers or step-counting devices. These should not be your sole measure for physical activity. There are also fitness apps you may find helpful. Some examples can be found in the Readings of Interest section of this chapter.

© Dudarev Mikhail/Shutterstock.com

Get started today on a route to physical fitness and maximizing your body's vitality. Staying motivated is key. Be sure you set goals, make physical fitness part of your life plan, track your progress, and if you can, exercise with a friend or colleague. Most of all, be flexible, stay on track, and have fun! It can only improve the quality of your daily life, help you achieve the *life you love,* and be one of the key elements to assist you in realizing your dreams. What a high to look in the mirror and see the results of just spending 2% of the 1440 minutes you have each day on physical fitness and exercise!

MINDFULNESS PRACTICE
USING THE MINDFUL MAC GUIDE

Mindful **MAC** Guide

The 4 Step MAC Guide will help you practice mindfulness.

1. Mindfully **acknowledge** an experience you had this week without internal or external filters
2. Intentionally pay **attention** to your senses, thoughts, emotions, and instincts regarding this experience
3. **Accept** the experience without judgment or expectations
4. **Choose** to respond versus reacting to the experience

Discuss how well you did with your practice this week, feelings you had, obstacles you faced and how you overcame them.

_____

_____

_____

_____

_____

_____

_____

_____

_____

_____

_____

_____

_____

_____

_____

_____

_____

_____

DESIGNER ACTIVITIES

Please answer the following:

1. Use words or draw a picture that would best describe what your body looks like to you. To others?

    _____

    _____

    _____

2. How would you describe your posture and body mechanics? What specifically would you do to improve one or both?

    _____

    _____

    _____

Timmy, stop being naughty: Don't sit up straight!

Cartoonstock.com

3. If you were to rate your physical literacy, what would that rating be. 10 is the highest and 1 is the lowest. What areas would you work on to bring your rating to a 10?

    _____

    _____

    _____

4. What forms of recreation do you do participate in regularly? If you don't participate, which would you like to pursue?

    _____

    _____

    _____

5. Do you play? If you do, describe what you do? If you don't what would you like to include as "play" in your life?

    _____

    _____

    _____

© Stefano Cavoretto/Shutterstock.com

6. What type(s) of physical activity do you participate in each week?

_____

_____

_____

7. If you already have an active physical fitness/activity plan, keep a journal of what you do, how often and how do you feel during and after exercising. Describe what keeps you physically active so you can remember that when you don't want to do it.

_____

_____

_____

8. If you are not physically active, list the types of activities you would like to do and then list what keeps you from doing them. Then describe ways in which you can decrease these potential barriers so you can start a fitness plan. Be sure to start with small realistic goals.

_____

_____

_____

9. If you know people who have been successful with a fitness plan, interview them and find out what motivated them to start and what keeps them "on track."

_____

_____

_____

10. If you are not able to be physically active due to a chronic or debilitating condition, describe ways in which you can maximize your body's vitality.

_____

_____

_____

LIFE BY PERSONAL DESIGN
REFLECTIVE JOURNAL

In this Reflective Journal, record what you learned from this chapter, your "intentions" for change, any barriers you think might interfere with these desired changes and how you will overcome them, and at least *one* strategy that will help you realize your dreams and the life you will love.

_____

_____

_____

_____

_____

_____

_____

_____

_____

_____

_____

_____

_____

_____

_____

_____

_____

_____

_____

_____

_____

_____

_____

_____

READINGS OF INTEREST

American Heart Association. (2016). Get moving. Easy tips to get active. http://www.heart.org/HEARTORG/HealthyLiving/PhysicalActivity/Physical-Activity_UCM_001080_SubHomePage.jsp

Aspen Institute. Project Play. (2015). Physical literacy in the US. A model, strategic plan, and call to action. http://aspenprojectplay.org/sites/default/files/PhysicalLiteracy_AspenInstitute.pdf Body Image Health. The Model for Healthy Body Image and Weight. http://bodyimagehealth.org/model-for-healthy-body-image/

Duffy, J. (2016, July 8). The 25 Best Fitness Apps of 2016. *PCMagazine*. http://www.pcmag.com/article2/0,2817,2485287,00.asp

NIH National Institute on Aging. Go4Life https://go4life.nia.nih.gov/

NIH Senior Health. Exercise: Benefits of exercise. https://nihseniorhealth.gov/exerciseforolderadults/healthbenefits/01.html

President's Council on Fitness, Sports & Nutrition. Sport for all initiative. http://www.fitness.gov/be-active/sport-for-all-initiative/

University of Michigan. University Health Services (2016). Computer ergonomics: How to protect yourself from strain and pain. https://www.uhs.umich.edu/computerergonomics

REFERENCES

1. Encyclopedia Britannica online. William Sheldon. https://www.britannica.com/biography/William-Sheldon

2. World Health Organization. International Travel and Health. http://www.who.int/ith/mode_of_travel/DVT/en/

3. Cornell University Ergonomics Web. CU Ergo. Sitting and Standing at Work. http://www.ergo.human.cornell.edu/CUESitStand.html

4. Environmental Health and Safety. University of Virginia. Ergonomics. Back Injury Prevention. http://ehs.virginia.edu/ehs/ehs.ergo/ergo.back.html

5. Baylor Health. What is Posture and Why Does it Matter? http://healthsource.baylorhealth.com/3,40037

6. Ayyappa, M.S. (1997). Normal human locomotion, Part 1: Basic concepts and terminology. *Journal of Prosthetics and Orthotics* 9(1), 10–17.

7. Joyner, J. (2015, December 23). At what age do most children start walking? Livestrong.com http://www.livestrong.com/article/522421-at-what-age-do-most-children-start-walking/

8. Allen, J. (2013, December 18). What is the difference between walking & running strides? Livestrong.com http://www.livestrong.com/article/364340-what-is-the-difference-between-walking-running-strides/

9. Mayo Clinic (2016). Fitness training: Elements of a well-rounded routine http://www.mayoclinic.org/healthy-lifestyle/fitness/in-depth/fitness-training/art-20044792?pg=1

10. HealthyPeople.gov. Healthy People 2020. Physical activity. https://www.healthypeople
    .gov/2020/topics-objectives/topic/physical-activity

11. The International Physical Literacy Association, (2014, May) Defining physical literacy.
    https://www.physical-literacy.org.uk/defining-physical-literacy/

12. Ferkel, R. C., Judge, L. W., Stodden, & D. F. Griffin, K. (2014). Importance of health-
    related fitness knowledge to increasing physical activity and physical fitness. *Physical
    Educator, 71*(2), 218–233.

13. Centers for Disease Control and Prevention. (2014). http://www.cdc.gov/physicalactivity/
    data/facts.htm

14. Lets Move.gov. http://www.letsmove.gov/

15. Hurd, A. R., & Anderson, D. H. (2011). Definitions of leisure, play, and recreation.
    Excerpt from *The Parks and Recreation Professional's Handbook.* http://www.humanki-
    netics.com/excerpts/excerpts/Definitions-of-Leisure-Play-and-Recreation

16. UNICEF. (2004). Sport, recreation, and play. http://www.unicef.org/ceecis/
    5571_SPORT_EN.pdf

17. SHAPE America. Fields of Study - Recreation and Leisure http://www.shapeamerica.org/
    career/fields/recreation-leisure.cfm

18. Owen, N., Sparling, P.B., Healy, G.N., Dunstan, D.W., & Matthews, C.E. (2010,
    December) Sedentary behavior: Emerging evidence for a new health risk, *Mayo
    Clinic Proceedings, 85*(12): 1138–1141.

19. HealthyPeople.gov. Healthy People 2020. Physical activity. https://www.healthypeople
    .gov/2020/topics-objectives/topic/physical-activity

20. Cherney, J. (2016). *Goals and Barriers Worksheet.* Phoenix: Body Definitions, LLC.

21. President's Council on Fitness, Sports, & Nutrition. Physical activity guidelines for
    Americans. http://www.fitness.gov/be-active/physical-activity-guidelines-for-americans/

22. Mayo Clinic. Fitness program: 5 steps to get started. http://www.mayoclinic.org/
    healthy-lifestyle/fitness/in-depth/fitness/art-20048269

23. American College of Sports Medicine. (2011, July). ACSM Issues New Recommendations
    on Quantity and Quality of Exercise. http://www.acsm.org/about-acsm/media-room/
    news-releases/2011/08/01/acsm-issues-new-recommendations-on-quantity-and-quality-
    of-exercise

24. Centers for Disease Control and Prevention. How much physical activity do adults need?
    http://www.cdc.gov/physicalactivity/basics/adults/index.htm
    Physical Activity and Health http://www.cdc.gov/physicalactivity/basics/pa-health/index.htm
    Measuring Physical Activity Intensity http://www.cdc.gov/physicalactivity/basics/
    measuring/index.html

25. NIH National Center for Complementary and Integrative Health. Complementary,
    Alternative, or Integrative Health: What's In a Name? https://nccih.nih.gov/health/
    integrative-health

26. Federal Trade Commission. (2012). Tips for buying exercise equipment.
    https://www.consumer.ftc.gov/articles/0051-tips-buying-exercise-equipment

CHAPTER 4

DISCOVERING YOUR BALANCE: REST AND RELAXATION

Photo courtesy of Marie Napoli

© Maria Napoli

Just sitting
Listening to the silence
Leaves rustling
Soft whispering wind
Sound of my breath

(Napoli)

LEARN TO BALANCE YOUR REST AND RELAXATION

- Become aware of the importance of relaxation
- Integrate personal relaxation strategies into your life
- Appreciate the benefits of rest
- Explore the significance of napping behaviors
- Become aware of the consequences of poor sleep habits
- Recognize what happens during sleep
- Incorporate healthy sleep behaviors
- Use the Mindful MAC Guide to balance rest and relaxation

This chapter focuses on rest and relaxation. Our daily lives consist of working, eating, shopping, caring for others, and technology stimulation often taking us away from these simple essentials. Can you honestly say that you have enough rest and relaxation in your life? If you are like most people living in a modern culture, probably not. Technology has offered us many benefits, having ready access to information and increased communication, yet your face-to-face time with one another and time for rest and relaxation and simple downtime is dwindling. Time that was once spent sharing communal space is rapidly being replaced by technology with people glued to social media, cell phone, and the Internet. A study of 10–17 year olds who had cell phones found that 52% sent text messages from a movie theatre; 96% communicated with their parents daily via cell phone; 28% sent messages from the dinner table; 33% would rather give up radio, video games or trips to the mall; 20% would give up television, and 25% would give up their MP3 players rather than give up their cell phones.[1]

In today's world people seem to be more stressed than ever. Life often feels complicated with juggling many activities at one time. Long gone are the days of just sitting either alone or with others in simple conversation. People are running at a faster pace in everything they do. Think about it for a moment. There are faster cars, the Internet, television, self-check-out stores, faster trains and planes, and walking for some has been replaced by motor scooters. If things are not happening at a fast pace, people are frequently frustrated, angry and even in a rage! Can we stop the madness and slow down? If not, stress is usually the outcome. The world has become addicted to stress hormones, fueling the fight or flight response. Unless a lion is chasing you, there is no reason to activate the sympathetic nervous system. There are many research studies that deal with the impact of stress on psychological, physical, and emotional health. Living in the parasympathetic system, the place of rest and healing while activating the relaxation response is where you want to spend most of your time.

Finding ways to calm the mind through mindfulness and relax the body are tools not to eliminate stress, but to help manage the effects of stress. The relaxation response has been one technique used for decades. "The relaxation response is the opposite of the stress response. It's a state of profound rest that can be elicited in many ways. With regular practice, you can create a well of calm to dive into as the need arises." Some relaxation techniques you might consider are: taking long slow deep breaths to disengage your mind from distracting thoughts, guided imagery by thinking about calming places or experiences, mindful meditation, bringing your attention to the present without drifting back in time or ahead into the future. Yoga, tai chi, and qigong are ancient practices that combine rhythmic breathing with a series of flowing body movements that activate the parasympathetic nervous system.[2] In spite of the lack of time people allocate for rest and relaxation, there are ways to reassess and begin to explore important activities that offer emotional, psychological, and physical well being.

Let's begin.

RELAXATION

Rest and relaxation can be experienced by doing absolutely nothing! This can be a rejuvenating experience; letting go of everything for a day. This is a great exercise to practice to fine tune your awareness. Here are some benefits you can give your body when you give it sufficient rest and relaxation:

- "Recharge your batteries" by sitting in nature. Activate your senses by listening to the birds singing, leaves crackling, and smelling the air.

- Clear your mind from the various "mindless monsters" that dictate the "shoulds and have-to's" offering your mind a rest from thoughts that consume you on a daily basis. As a result, you may feel less anxious and distracted and experience more joy and focus.

- Find ways to explore activities that bring laughter and calmness.

Let's take a closer look at ways you can introduce rest and relaxation into your life. The fact of the matter is, the activity of incorporating rest and relaxation is quite simple and has ample benefits.

LISTEN TO THE SILENCE

When you think about relaxation, does silence come to mind? Maybe not, yet in a world where noise floods us, we have invented ways to quiet "noise pollution" that disturbs peace. Some are noise canceling headphones, soundproof rooms, and silent meditation courses. Just look at signs in hospitals and offices that say "Quiet Please." Do you know that the word *noise* is derived from the Latin root meaning queasiness or pain? A correlation has been found between noise and sleep loss, heart disease and tinnitus (ringing or buzzing in the ear). There is an interesting physiological process of how the body interprets noise. First, when noise is heard and identified, your amygdala, the part of the brain associated with memory and emotion, is activated, which then triggers a release of stress hormones.[3] You learned from previous discussions about stress hormones such as cortisol and norepinephrine. They signal the "fight or flight" response, which places your body in reactive versus responsive mode.

Practicing silence often has a negative connotation. For example, people who are generally quiet may be given a label of being shy or aloof as engaging in conversation when people are together is expected. When people feel rejected phrases such as "getting the silent treatment" or "so and so is not speaking to me" have negative inferences.[4] Sometimes, people may simply not want to engage in conversation, but rather want to observe or actively listen. An interesting piece of information about silence was found studying auditory stimuli and mice. The mice were exposed to various auditory stimuli such as music, a baby mouse call, white noise, and silence with the expectation that the baby mouse calls would facilitate new brain cells. Surprisingly, these sounds only produced short-term neurological effects. Two hours of silence per day promoted cell development in their hippocampus, the region in your brain related to memory and senses.[5] What does this mean? You can actually generate new brain cells by practicing silence! "If we can find the courage to sit quietly with gently closed eyes, giving ourselves the permission to leave the outer world and enter our inner one, our thoughts will settle and our minds will become clear. It is in this stillness, and solitude that the potential harmony of the heart and mind reside."[6] Try observing silence for a day, or a few hours in a day. Pay attention to your experience. You may see the world through a very different lens.

© pkchai/Shutterstock.com

MUSIC—WINDOW TO THE SOUL

Music has historically been an avenue recognized for calming and relaxation. Parents singing soft lullabies to a child, teenagers lying on their beds listening to their favorite songs, adults swaying in an intimate slow dance, listening to music as you cook or read to facilitate focus are some ways music has been found to bring relaxation. Although this is not new information, research has recently confirmed how music impacts the nervous system. Most of us enjoy one form of music, generally finding the experience pleasurable. Listening to music requires active listening, alertness and attention. Some interesting research has explored the physiological response to music and how it pertains to arousal and relaxation. When the brain is alerted to sound, the neurons in the auditory cortex light up and if the sounds continue in a constant pattern, the neurons generally stop reacting. Simply stated, the intelligence of the neurons communicate when they notice a change in input. In regard to how this pattern relates to one listening to music, it was found that if one listened to a musical track, and random stretches of silence were inserted into the music, it was found to be relaxing. It was even more relaxing when two-minute silent pauses were inserted. In conclusion, during faster rhythms one activates concentrated attention and relaxation during pauses or slower rhythms.[7] What type of music activates the relaxation response? You might wonder if listening to loud screaming music that many teenagers are drawn to activates the sympathetic or parasympathetic nervous system.

Young adult women were randomly assigned to three different types of music prior to taking a stress test; a) relaxing music (RM) {Misere'Allegri) b) sounds of rippling water (SW) and c) rest (R) without acoustic stimulation. Although it was hypothesized that listening to the relaxing music (RM) before a stress test would result in a decreased stress response the study found that the sounds of rippling water (SW) actually had the lowest cortisol response and relaxing music (RM) had the highest cortisol response.[8]

Examining these findings may mean that one may predict what has been known intuitively—that sounds in nature elicit relaxation. Also, based on the research done by Bernardi, when a person listens to sounds of rippling water, those sounds may be constant and repetitive with little change and long stretches of silence, which were found to be relaxing; they did not activate the neurons which react to change. In another study, following a stressful arithmetic task, where skin conductance levels were used to index sympathetic activation and high frequency heart rate variability to index parasympathetic activation, there were no effects on the high frequency heart rate variability, but skin conductance levels recovery tended to be faster during natural sounds than noisy environments.[9]

Due to the relaxation music can provide, it is no surprise that music can help with insomnia, anxiety, and depression. In a study, patients suffering from posttraumatic stress disorder with insomnia were exposed to a muscle relaxation CD and music relaxation CD. Results of the study found that music relaxation was effective in that it led to significant improvements in sleep and decreased depression. It is interesting to note the type of music used during this intervention: a slow melody with minor harmony played on a piano and background violins and bells played slowly over ten minutes with the melody repeated four times.[10] When reflecting upon the research discussed above where neurons do not light up if there is little change activating the parasympathetic nervous system, it can be seen that repetition of sounds with little change may induce relaxation as the brain is not alerted to change.

As you begin to choose music as a relaxation activity, you might consider the type of music that can activate the relaxation response. Better yet, think about the natural sounds of nature as your favorite form of music as a way to add to sound, senses, and physical calm. Listen and enjoy!

HAVE A GOOD LAUGH

"Time spent laughing is time spent with the gods."[11]

One cannot forget the importance of laughter when adding rest and relaxation into your life "Laughter is a complex human behavior, with inherent characteristics involving and reflecting participation of almost every functional element of the human organism, is ubiquitous in the human world population and no human group has been identified as being devoid of laughter."[12]

© Sergey Furtaev/Shutterstock.com

The physiological systems involved in humor, mirth, and laughter involve the muscular, cardiovascular, respiratory, endocrine, immune, and central nervous systems. Laughter has the following impact:

1. Exercises and relaxes muscles
2. Improves respiration
3. Stimulates circulation
4. Decreases stress hormones
5. Increases the immune system's defenses
6. Elevates pain threshold and tolerance
7. Enhances mental functioning.

Think of the feelings you have after a good laugh. Laughter has both short term and long-term benefits. "In the short term, a bout of laughter appears to initiate the stress response, with a slight increase in heart rate, blood pressure, muscle tension, and ventilations. But this is quickly followed by a rebound effect, where these parameters decrease to below previous resting levels. The overall effect is a profound level of homeostasis and an immune system boost. Laughter is also credited with stabilizing blood pressure, 'massaging' vital organs, stimulating circulation, facilitating digestion and increasing oxygenated blood throughout the body."[13] When children play, you usually hear laughter. Norman Cousins discusses how he cured himself of a terminal illness by making sure he spent many hours a day laughing in his book *Anatomy of an Illness*. Your entire body responds and tingles in a good way.

In general, laughter has been found to have physiological, psychological, and social and quality of life benefits with limited adverse effects. A study on the effect of mirthful laughter on the vascular system found that volunteers who watched a movie or segment of popular comedies, for example Saturday Night Live, had improved vasculature (arrangement of blood vessels in your organs) resulting from mirthful laughter compared to those who viewed movies that elicit mental stress such as *Saving Private Ryan*. As a result of this study, one might conclude that the reduction of vascular inflammation with mirthful laughter may serve as a useful and important vehicle for vascular health.[14] Patients experiencing radiation therapy for breast cancer were found to reduce anxiety, depression, and stress following only one session of a therapeutic laughter program.[15] Based on the many positive effects laughter can offer you in your daily life, it makes sense to add laughter to your daily diet of healthy activities. This is one activity you do not have to pay for or go anywhere to reap the benefits. As far as it is known, there are relatively no negative side effects to laughter or added calories so why not increase and indulge!

ESSENTIAL OILS, SENSE, AND SCENT

© Lukas Gojda/Shutterstock.com

Enjoying the scent of essential oils to enhance relaxation is a delicious experience. There are many scents to choose from to add extra quality to your life. For example, tangerine, lavender, ylang ylang, geranium, and jasmine aid in stimulating relaxation. You can use them in a diffuser, in your bath, or dab a small amount on your forehead or behind your ears. One of the most popular oils that activate relaxation is lavender. Koulivand, Ghadiri and Gorji's article on lavender and the nervous system explored the existing research documenting the many benefits of lavender on the nervous system. Lavender was found to reduce anxiety and improve symptoms associated with anxiety such as restlessness, disturbed sleep and somatic complaints, and, in general, improved well being and quality of life. Lavender was also found to have an antidepressant effect as well as minimizing the side effects of imipramine such as dry mouth and urinary retention.[16] Essential oils are frequently used by massage therapists. A study of massage recipients using lavender found they were less anxious and more positive than those who only had a massage without the oil. When inhaled, lavender has been found to have a calming, soothing, and sedative effect.[17]

One of the most debilitating problems affecting thousands of people worldwide is insomnia. While this will be discussed later in the chapter, it is relevant to point out that lavender has been found to be effective as a natural remedy to treat insomnia and improve sleep quality. Mixing lavender, basil, juniper, and sweet marjoram has also been found to reduce sleep disturbance.[18] When you are looking for a relaxing experience that smells good too, try dabbing a few drops of lavender oil behind your ears. Take a mini vacation for one minute and simply breathe in the scent.

POWER OF THE BREATH

© Emilie Gerard/Shutterstock.com

You may often find yourself saying, "I do not have time to relax." Breathing is the only autonomic function we have; it usually works on its own without conscious awareness, but if you bring attention to your breath, which is already happening on its own, you can change the entire experience. When you are mindful and pay attention to your breath, you activate the relaxation response. Mindful breathing is simply the act of noticing your breath, paying attention to the thoughts that arise, letting them go, and continuing with focused attention to your breath. In a study of female undergraduate students, the effects of mindful breathing, progressive muscle relaxation, and loving kindness meditation were compared to determine the frequency of repetitive thoughts during the exercise. It was found that the mindful breathing participants reported greater decentering and less repetitive thoughts compared with the progressive muscle relaxation and loving kindness meditation.[19]

Based on the findings of this study, mindful breathing may be a helpful tool to quiet the "mindless monster" of intrusive thoughts as well as an effective strategy to manage stress. Here is an activity you can try.

Mindful three-part belly breath

1. Get comfortable. Sit with your back straight and chest lifted. Alternatively you can lie down on your back.
2. Slowly take a breath in through your nose.
3. Notice how the breath moves from you lungs to your tummy, ribs, chest, and shoulders. Notice your belly filling up like a balloon.
4. Exhale by letting the breath ooze out of your lungs slowly like a balloon losing its air until empty.
5. Notice any thoughts that arise.
6. Continue with the breath, paying attention to the experience.

Let's now look at the benefits of various breathing practices. The Ujjayi breath often called the "Ocean breath" has been found to increase parasympathetic activity through slow breath rate, contraction of the laryngeal musculature, inspiration against airway resistance, prolonged expiration against airway resistance, and breath hold. A study of 70 college students found that this slow breathing with prolonged expiration was shown to reduce psychological and physiological arousal in an anxiety-provoking situation. In addition, the Ujjayi breathing improved heart rate variability, quieted the mind, and may stabilize the cortex through an increase of gamma-aminobutyric acid (GABA), an inhibitory neurotransmitter that has a calming effect on the brain and body.[20] Take a moment and experience the Ujjayi Ocean breath and notice the feeling of calm.

Practice the Ocean Breath!

1. Get comfortable; sit with your back straight and chest lifted. Alternatively you can lie down on your back.
2. As you slowly take a breath in through your nose, let the breath out keeping your mouth closed making a long *ahhhhhhhhhhhh* sound. (Feel the back of your throat gently pushing your breath while making this ocean sound).
3. Try taking in longer breaths and make you exhalations while remaining in a comfortable position.
4. Listen to your personal ocean, imagine your own boat, and let the waves sweep you away.

Ancient teachings tell us that "he who learns how to breathe like a baby becomes immortal."[21] Now that you have taken the time to experience your breath in a very different way you will begin to see changes in your everyday experiences.

MINDFUL MEDITATION

"Most people agree that being in the present moment is desirable but they cannot find the way to get there."[22] Many of you may have tried meditation and found that you were easily distracted. Beginning meditators report that they are distracted by thoughts, feelings, sounds, or physical sensations. Studies have shown that mindfulness increases emotion regulation, reduces reactivity to emotional stimuli, and increases the tolerance and willingness to be exposed to negative stimuli.[23] Regardless of the amount of distracting thoughts or emotions that arise during meditation, your ability to notice them and not get stuck dwelling on or trying to dismiss them is the key to continuing with your mindful meditation practice.

Also, there are myths about meditation that say you must sit in a particular position, feel a certain way, and have enlightened outcomes. Mindful meditation is one of the simplest forms of meditation as there are no requirements other than observing and paying attention to your experience. There is no expectation to change your experience, as it is happening anyway. When you bring conscious attention to your experience awareness increases. Since mindful meditation has been shown to be a buffer against the long-term wear and tear effects of stress, you may increase your telomere length, hence, reducing stress and slowing down the aging process. Telomeres are the caps at the end of each strand of DNA that protect our chromosomes, like the plastic tips at the end of shoelaces.[24] Without the coating, shoelaces become frayed until they can no longer do their job, just as without telomeres. DNA strands become damaged and the cells can't do their job. Physiologically speaking, shorter telomere length is related to poor quality of health and aging. When you are in a stressful state, and activate your stress hormones of cortisol and catecholamine you are more prone to shorter telomeres. Furthermore, there is a link between stress arousal and oxidative stress and telomere shortness, as meditation seems to improve the endocrine balance by lowering cortisol and decreasing oxidative stress. As a result, the more you practice meditation, the more you may promote mitotic cell longevity by decreasing your stress hormones and oxidative stress and increasing those hormones that can protect the telomere.[25] As you begin your mindful meditation practice, take a moment to set the stage for acceptance of and openness to your experience. The fact of the matter is, it is your experience; embrace it, learn from it and let go. The more you can to let go, the more you will create opportunities for relaxation.

MINDFUL MEDITATION GUIDE

Find a comfortable place to sit preferably upright

Begin focusing on your breathing (notice the tip of your nose)

Notice your experience, body sensations, smells, thoughts, and emotions

Accept your experience without judgment. Do not try to change anything

(Remember, thoughts and emotions will arise. Allow them to emerge and let them flow by)

Continue focusing on your breath and whatever experience you are having

Reflect upon your experience

YOGA—STRETCH INTO BLISS

© Wehands/Shutterstock.com

The word *yoga* in Sanskrit, which is spelled "yuj" means union or join and to direct and concentrate one's attention. "According to ancient Vedic texts the aim of yoga was to 'cut the seed of sorrow' before it sprouts."[26] When you think about yoga you may visualize a person moving in a posture or pose, called *asana*. The fact of the matter is the practice of yoga is much more than an exercise. Yoga is a lifestyle involving conscious breathing, meditation, healthy diet, and self-reflection, maintaining a positive mind, healing oneself from within, and being an active participant in maintaining a quality of life. These are a few of the teachings of the classic text as described by Pantajali, an eightfold path to awareness and enlightenment.[27] Practicing yoga has many benefits both physical and emotional. Due to the relaxation achieved by activating the parasympathetic nervous system, yoga has been found to calm the mind, relieve insomnia, decrease the amount of time needed to fall asleep, increase the number of hours slept, and can bring about a feeling of being rested in the morning.[28] Research findings have shown that participant heart rate increased while engaged in yoga postures and decreased in guided relaxation and after cyclic meditation. Another study found that there is an increase in sympathetic activation during the practice of yoga postures and increase of parasympathetic activity in cyclic meditation, which offers a balance of exercise, and relaxation in these activities.[29] Yoga has been found to have an immediate quieting effect on the sympathetic nervous system/HPA axis response to stress. Although walking and stretching was found to make subjects in the study feel better, those who practiced yoga and breathing seemed to have an improvement in relieving physical symptoms and perceptions of stress. In general, the research on healthy individuals comparing exercise (walking, biking, etc) to yoga has shown that practicing yoga is as effective or superior to exercise.[30]

Everyone needs to exercise on a regular basis as you read in chapter 3. It is essential to good health. Adding the practice of yoga is a huge bonus as the benefits achieved go beyond physical. In addition to increasing energy, toning the body, increasing muscle strength, yoga offers a deep feeling of relaxation. Practicing yoga is a precious gift that can be appreciated at any age or physical situation.

Photo courtesy of Maria Napoli

NATURE—EXQUISITELY SIMPLE

In closing the discussion on relaxation, let's turn to nature to provide more food for your soul. As discussed thus far, people are often moving so fast they miss the obvious. How often do you connect with nature? When you walk down the street do you notice a tree swaying in the wind, smell a flower, listen to a bird singing, watch a sunset, or simply gaze at whatever comes your way? Sometimes people think they need to go on a vacation to enjoy nature without considering or taking the time to realize that nature is all around you. Even city life can provide the serenity of nature. The sky is always there whether it be sunny, cloudy, or misty. Listening to the rain against the window, or better yet, walking in the rain and feeling the drops wash over you can be invigorating. The benefits you receive from nature contribute to your quality of life in every aspect of living. How are you engaged with nature? Think about where you live, work, and play. Are you paying attention? If not take a moment to visualize where you live. Write down how you experience your connection with nature, whether you are walking, sitting, running, or driving in your car. Remember to breathe as you take in this beauty that surrounds you and pay attention to your experience.

© shutt2016/Shutterstock.com

REST

Every living being needs to sleep. Sleeping occurs every day yet not much thought is given to it. Recently, it was found that when people sleep there is a lot going on besides dreaming. Of course, getting enough sleep is vital for maintaining good health. Sleep is as important to good health as oxygen. Our nervous system depends upon us getting enough sleep to work properly. Surprisingly, even a slight deprivation of night's sleep can negatively effect one's health. In fact, sleep is one of the most important aspects of our lives that either contributes to our good health or increases mortality! Some get enough sleep, yet others are sleep deprived and need to nap during the day. "Age has a lot to do with how much sleep people need. Babies need 16–18 hours of sleep, pre school children 11–12 hours, school aged children, 10 hours, teens 9–10 hours, and adults and older adults 7–8 hours a day."[31] As you can see, the amount of sleep needed for good health is not the five or six hours that many have and think is enough. Some may believe they are losing out on activities if they sleep too much. Others are unable to get to sleep due to insomnia, medications, work schedules, anxiety, depression, or medical conditions interfering with their sleep cycle. Napping can help when one does not get enough sleep. However, depending on napping to help catch up on sleep on a regular basis does not take the place of a good night's sleep. Infants and children need to nap during the day as well as have many hours of sleep at night. Have you ever followed a toddler around even for one hour? There is a story about a football player who thought he could keep up with his toddler. He did everything his toddler did and after an hour gave up feeling exhausted! Children expend a lot of physical energy and need sleep as they are still growing and their bodies need this opportunity to support that growth. Let's take a look at what the research has found about napping and sleep.

NAPPING

Napping is typical for babies, yet many adults take naps for different reasons. For example, in warmer climates people take siestas. A large meal is eaten in the afternoon and taking a nap is part of that ritual. As mentioned, babies nap for longer periods of time; adults nap less but as people age they begin to nap more. A study exploring the benefits of napping for younger, middle-aged, and older adults hypothesized that older adults needed longer naps since they expe-

© Voyagerix/Shutterstock.com

rience less restorative benefits than their younger counterparts do. It was also found that older adults are able to achieve as much benefit from a nap as their younger counterparts but they had to work harder to realize the same results on performance tests.[32] All of us at one time have experienced exhaustion and fatigue from lack of sleep or from over activity, which may or may not include work. When people are sleep deprived, taking a nap can be refreshing, mood enhancing, and aid in performing tasks requiring reasoning and quick reaction time. If you are sleep deprived, your safety could be at risk. Often people feel sleepy after lunch. When employees had a nap after their post lunch lag they improved their performance and alertness.[33]

There are many theories about how long one should nap for it to be beneficial. Can one achieve benefit after a ten-minute nap? Is an hour or two hours too long? If you are getting enough sleep, seven to nine hours, you will not need a long nap to improve alertness, yet if you are sleep deprived, longer naps are more beneficial. Male and female university students in their twenties who were good sleepers participated in assessing the benefits of no nap, a 10-minute, and a 30-minute nap. They reported that immediately following a 10-minute nap they were more alert and had improved cognitive performance based on two instruments assessing cognition. (Symbol-Digit Substitution Task—a series of nine novel shapes paired with digits between one and nine where participants were asked to copy corresponding digits from a long random sequence of shapes.) and Letter Cancellation Task (participants searched for two target letters in a matrix of alphanumeric stimuli, and scored on the number of correct identification in a four-minute period). Interestingly, 35 minutes after the 10-minute nap there was only an advantage on a Letter Cancellation measure, yet one hour after napping students reported comparable alertness for the 10 and 30 minute nap, which was much greater than no napping.[34]

It has been found that longer napping is not recommended as it produces more sleep inertia, where one may experience confusion, grogginess and some impairment in cognitive ability to think clearly. A study examining the health relevance of napping in 34–82 year olds found three patterns of nappers: infrequent nappers with a good night time sleep, frequent nappers with a good night time sleep, and nappers with a poor nighttime sleep. Those who had poor night time sleep showed elevated noradrenaline levels, depressive symptoms, and perceived stress scores compared to the other two groups of nappers.[35]

People all over the world nap. In regard to napping, when one naps, how long and the age of the napper are important factors to consider when assessing the benefits of a nap.[36] Regardless of when and how long one naps, getting a good night's sleep is still always a prerequisite for achieving the best results from napping.

© Ollyy/Shutterstock.com

SLEEP

Like breathing, sleep is something you do every day but may not give a lot of thought to. Over one billion people on planet Earth are sleeping every day, yet only recently have the benefits of getting enough sleep and the negative impact of sleep deprivation been identified. What happens while you sleep directly impacts what will happen during the day? With increased technology, sededentary patterns of behavior, stress, and emotional problems such as anxiety and depression, people are having difficulty sleeping. Students who were sleep deprived, had erratic sleep/wake schedules, late bed and rise times, and poor sleep quality experienced poor school performance as teens and through college. Lack of adequate sleep impacts brain function, therefore, it is no surprise that academic performance is affected by poor sleep quality. The American Academy of Sleep Medicine suggests that students can improve the quality of their sleep if they go bed early and get out of bed and do something relaxing if they cannot fall asleep. It is also suggested that your bed be used for sleeping and not for studying, phone calls, or watching TV. It is further suggested that you take only short naps, less than an hour and before 3pm; wake up on the weekends at the same time as school or work days; avoid caffeine; keep the room dark; do something relaxing before going to bed; and do not eat before going to bed.[37]

Falling asleep, getting up during sleep, racing thoughts, noise and air quality are just some obstacles impairing sleep quality. Getting enough sleep or sleeping too much can even increase how long you live! A meta-analysis of 16 sleep studies with over a thousand men and women found that both short and long durations of sleep are significant predictors of death. The following patterns of sleep regardless of gender or socioeconomic status found that; short sleepers (less than 7 often less than 5 hours) have a 12% risk of dying compared with long sleepers (more than 8 or 9 hours) who have a 30% greater risk of dying than those sleeping 7–8 hours a night.[38] One may be surprised to know that sleeping too much as well as not getting enough sleep is a serious risk to one's mortality. Getting enough sleep (8–9 hour a night) improves learning and memory, stabilizes metabolism and weight, increases safety from accidents due to sleepiness, and maintains decreased stress hormone levels and normal heartbeat while improving immune function.[39]

How does a lack of sleep contribute to disease? Shockingly, a well-known study of rats reported that when they were sleep deprived they died within three weeks.[40] Here are some examples of the effects of sleep deprivation on the body and its influence on health issues.

"What's holding him up?"

HEALTH ISSUES	EFFECT OF SLEEP DEPRIVATION
Obesity	Sleep causes the body to secrete hormones to control appetite, energy metabolism and glucose processing.
Diabetes	Sleep influences how the body processes glucose, high energy carbohydrate cells used for fuel
Heart disease/ hypertension	People with hypertension may experience elevated blood pressure; increase risk of cardiovascular disease and stroke
Sleep apnea	Frequent awakening causes brief surges in blood pressure
Mood disorders	Lack of sleep causes irritability, mental exhaustion, stress, anger, and sadness
Immune system	Better able to fight infection with adequate sleep
Alcohol	Often used for insomnia as a sedative but after a few hours, alcohol stimulates arousal causing one to awake
Life expectancy	Poor sleep is associated lower life expectancy[41]

Falling asleep and staying asleep are two issues that must be achieved for quality sleep. A study of individuals who had insomnia and normal sleepers found that both groups had similar ideas of what constituted good sleep quality, but those with insomnia had a long laundry list of requirements that defined quality sleep.[42] One may hypothesize that those who experience insomnia may, in general, be more rigid and/or anxious and need to adhere to regimens and expectations, which are brought to bed with them at night.

Sleep apnea can also interfere with sleep quality, particularly if it is not treated with a sleep apnea machine. Not only is there an interference with sleep, it can be dangerous when one stops breathing.

It is interesting that if you are able to wake up on your own you may be more alert than those who need an assist to wake up such as using alarms, even after being sleep deprived. A study assessing the effects of self-awakening on both morning and daytime alertness, after partial sleep deprivation, found that in the morning and during the day those who were able to self-awake were more alert and alleviated daytime sleepiness than those who needed forced awakening.[43] One may speculate that those who are able to self-awake have had consistency in sleep patterns and those who required a forced awakening may not have consistent sleep patterns or experience shorter sleep patterns.

Some people feel grouchy following a poor night's sleep and may be somewhat challenging to deal with during their first communication with others. How people interact is also impacted by sleep deprivation. They may just tune out their sensitivity to emotional information. A study assessing emotional empathy revealed that after a night of sleep deprivation, participants who were sleep deprived were less emotionally empathetic than those who had slept.[44] You are interacting with people all the time; at work, with your children, partners, friends, and strangers. Thinking about how sleep can impact how you relate to others and how aware and sensitive you are to other's feelings can change how you show up in your relationships.

Sometimes work schedules can interfere with quality of sleep. Nurses, firefighters, doctors, police, manufacturing, and emergency workers all have schedules that impact sleep. Yet these professionals are working in environments that directly impact others' lives and safety and therefore needs focused attention. Although many professions require fluctuating schedules that change often, and ones where they have to wake up for emergencies, research shows the importance of creating work schedules to optimize sleep before, sometime during, and after work. Work-sleep balance is as important as work-life balance.[45] One suggestion that has been made is to regularly incorporate recovery sleep time if sleep deprivation occurs more than one or two times during the week.

It is now apparent that sleep is an essential and important body function. Let's review what actually happens when you sleep. Your body is a mean machine and has its own internal body clock repeating a 24-hour rhythm called circadian rhythm. The longer you are awake, the more pressure there is for sleep to occur, generally peaking at night. Also, while you are awake, the compound adenosine continues to rise, which signals your body to prepare to sleep. When you are sleeping, adenosine breaks down preparing your body to wake up and start all over again. Another factor in your internal clock is the environment; light alerts the eyes that it is daytime. For those sleeping at night when it gets dark, the hormone melatonin is released signaling your body that its time to prepare to sleep and helps you feel drowsy. When the sun rises, your body releases cortisol preparing your body to wake up.[46]

There are basically two cycles of sleep: non-rapid eye movement (NREM) commonly known as deep sleep or slow wave sleep which generally makes up 75–80% of your sleep). During this cycle, your body is working. It is repairing itself by tissue growth and repair, energy restoration, and releasing hormones that are essential for growth and development. The remaining 20–25% of your sleep cycle is rapid-eye movement (REM). This is when dreaming happens and the time our minds are processing and consolidating emotions, memories, and stress.[47]

One might say that your body is first repairing and then processing emotions, memories, and stress, two very important functions for living a quality life. To function properly, your body needs to experience the full sleep cycle to prepare you for the next day feeling rejuvenated and regenerated. A survey indicated the following are important sleep aids. Check the ones that are important to you and add others than help you sleep. What makes a good night's sleep, National sleep Foundation.[48] (https://sleepfoundation.org/heathy-sleep-tips)

SLEEP AIDS	MY SLEEP AIDS
Comfortable mattress	
Comfortable pillows	
Comfortable sheets and bedding	
Quiet room	
Dark room	
Cool room temperature	
Fresh air	
Clean bedroom	
Relaxing bath or shower	
Prescription or over counter medication	
Other	
Other	

By now you realize the importance of getting a good night's sleep. The benefits that occur during sleep will impact everything that happens to you when you are awake. If you are not getting enough sleep, it is time to revisit your sleeping habits. If you are getting enough sleep, you may want to think about how you can sustain these good habits. Sleeping is a universal activity that supports good physical and emotional health, can improve your relationships as you are more aware of other's feelings, increases safety while driving and in the workplace by improved alertness, reduces the possibility of obesity, and most important, puts a smile on your face as you wake up refreshed and ready to engage in another amazing day of your life!

MINDFULNESS PRACTICE USING THE MINDFUL MAC GUIDE

Mindful **MAC** Guide

1. Mindfully **acknowledge** each experience without internal or external filters
2. Intentionally pay **attention** to your senses, thoughts, emotions, and instincts regarding each experience
3. **Accept** your experience without judgment or expectations
4. **Choose** to respond versus react to your experience

Discuss how well you did with your practice this week, feelings you had, obstacles you faced and how you overcame them.

_____

_____

_____

_____

_____

_____

_____

_____

_____

_____

_____

_____

_____

_____

_____

_____

_____

_____

_____

_____

_____

_____

DESIGNER ACTIVITIES

Please answer the following:

1. How often do you get 8-9 hours of sleep per night? If you are not getting enough sleep, what do you experience?

   _____

   _____

   _____

   _____

2. What are the ways in which you experience relaxation? If you are not getting enough, what prevents you from relaxing?

   _____

   _____

   _____

   _____

3. Do you feel that you laugh enough? If you do, describe your experience. If not, what gets in the way?

   _____

   _____

   _____

   _____

4. **Meditation**

   - Locate a space where you will not be interrupted
   - Find a sitting position that is comfortable
   - Pay attention to your breath
   - Scan your body with each breath and release any tension you are aware of
   - Continue focusing on the breath
   - Very gently rock back and forth. Pay attention only to the rocking
   - If you are interrupted by thoughts, acknowledge them and let them go without judgment
   - What are you aware of?

Imagery

- Pay attention to your breath
- Imagine a place in your mind that is peaceful and nurturing
- Allow yourself to explore
- Notice the experience of your senses; sight, sound, smell, taste, body and environmental temperature
- Notice the feelings that arise
- Continue to pay attention to the breath

Cobra Stretch Pose

- Lie down on your belly
- Take a few breaths
- Place your hands on the floor a few inches above your shoulders
- Press your pelvis gently into the floor
- Without pressing into your hands lift your chest with the energy of your breath. Do this a few times
- Now press your hands into the floor and lift your chest (you will notice a slight squeeze in the buttocks, which will protect your lower back)
- Come up to your full extension, your edge
- Breathe and come down slowly breathing all the way down
- Rest and relax

Relaxation Pose

- Position yourself onto your back
- Allow your body to find a comfortable position. Use a pillow or blanket, if needed
- Bring your arms out to a "T"
- Let your legs and feet relax
- Put your mind into your shoulders and hands
- Imagine and experience them becoming heavy, relaxed and warm
- Close your eyes
- Pay attention to your breath
- Rest & relax

Aromatherapy

- Run a warm bath
- Combine tangerine, lavender, and geranium oil
- Play your favorite soothing music
- Notice your breath
- Soak for 30–45 minutes
- Enjoy the scents
- Think positive thoughts

Play

- Find a friend to join you in a game (board game, sport, etc.)
- Allow yourself to immerse yourself in the experience with no expectations

Notice the experience of your thoughts, body, and emotions

Laughter

Watch your favorite comedy movie or show and observe how you feel when you laugh.

© AlbertLin/Shutterstock.com

Body _____

Attitude _____

Mind _____

Napping

Do you take naps during the day? If so, what time and how long?

© Javier Brosch/Shutterstock.com

_____

_____

_____

If you are napping during the day and your naps are 30 minutes or less how do you feel after napping?

_____

_____

_____

_____

If you are napping longer than one hour do you feel refreshed or do you experience drowsiness or brain fog? Also, if you are napping more than one hour does it interfere with getting to sleep at night or waking up during the night?

_____

_____

_____

_____

Sleep
Describe your ritual before going to sleep?

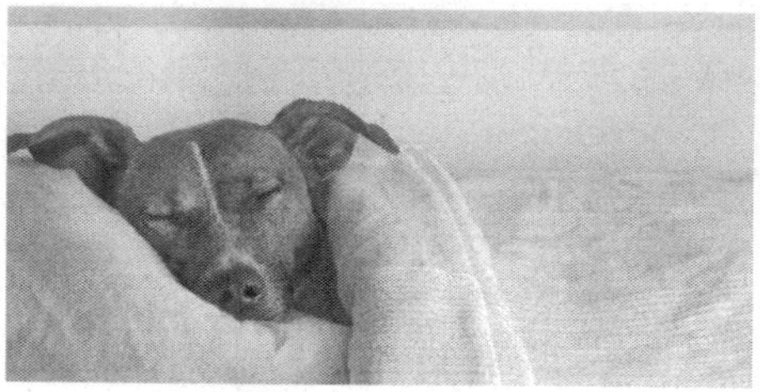

_____

_____

_____

_____

If this ritual works for you and you are getting 7–8 hours of sleep, describe how it is working for you. If it is not working, describe.

Describe how you feel after sleeping 7–8 hours

_____

_____

_____

_____

LIFE BY PERSONAL DESIGN
REFLECTIVE JOURNAL

In this Reflective Journal, record what you learned from this chapter, your "intentions" for change, any barriers you think might interfere with these desired changes and how you will overcome them, and at least *one* strategy that will help you realize your dreams and the life you will love.

_____

_____

_____

_____

_____

_____

_____

_____

_____

_____

_____

_____

_____

_____

_____

_____

_____

_____

_____

_____

_____

_____

_____

REFERENCES

1. Carr, E. R. (2007). Quality of life for our patients: How media images and messages influence their perceptions. *Clinical Journal of Oncology Nursing 12*, 43–51.

2. Harvard Medical School. (2016, September). Six relaxation techniques to reduce stress. *Harvard Health Publications: Harvard Medical School.* http://www.health.harvard.edu/mind-and-mood/six-relaxation-techniques-to-reduce-stress.

3. Gross, D. A. (2014, August). This is your brain on silence. *Nautilus, Nothingness Issue 16.*

4. Oppawsky, J. (2016, March). Silence is a counseling skill. *The Journal of the American Association of Integrative Medicine.*

5. Kirste, L., Nicola, Z., Kronenberg, G., Walker, T. L., Liu, R. C., & Kempermann, G. (2015). Is silence golden? Effects of auditory stimuli and their absence on adult hippocampal neurogenesis. *Brain Structure and Function. March 220 (2),*1221–8.

6. Siegel, N. (2007). Silence for renewal: The power of silence in the classroom. *The Lookstein Center for Jewish Education School of Education. Bar Ilan University Journal*

7. Bernardi, L., Porta, C., & Sleight, P. (2006). Cardiovascular, cerebrovascular and respiratory changes induced by different types of music in musicians and non-musicians: The importance of silence. *Heart, 92,* 445–452.

8. Thoma, M. V., La Marca, R., Bronnimann, R., Finkel, L., Ehlert, U., & Nater, U. M. (2013). The effect of music on the human stress response. *PLoS ONE 8 (8),*1–12.

9. Alvarsson, J., Wiens, S., & Nilsson, M. (2010, March). Stress recovery during exposure to nature sound and environmental noise. *International Journal of Environmental research and Public Health 7 (3),* 1036–46.

10. Blanaru, M., Bloch, B., Vadas, L., Arnon, Z., Ziv, N., Kremer, I., & Haimov, I. (2012). The Effects of music relaxation and muscle relaxation techniques on sleep quality and emotional measures among individuals with posttraumatic stress disorder. *Mental Illness, 4:e13.*

11. Dyer, W. W. (1998). *Wisdom of the Ages: A modern master brings eternal truths into everyday life.* NY: Harper Collins, 176.

12. Miller, M. and Fry, W. F. (2009).The effect of mirthful laughter on the human cardiovascular system. *Medical Hypotheses 73,* 636–639, 636

13. Seaward, B. L. (2006). *Managing stress: Principles and strategies for health and well being.* Sudbury, MA: Jones and Bartlett publishers, 271

14. Miller, M., & Fry, W. F. (2009). The effect of mirthful laughter on the human cardiovascular system. *Medical Hypotheses 73,* 636

15. Kim, S., Kim, Y. H., & Kim, H. J. (2015). Laughter and stress relief in cancer patients: A pilot study. *Evidence-Based Complimentary and Alternative Medicine 2015* **Identifiers:**pmc: PMC4439472, doi: 10.1155/2015/864739

16. Koulivand, P. H., Ghadiri, M. K., & Gorji, A. (2013). Lavender and the nervous system. *Evidence-Based Complementary and Alternative Medicine.* **http://**dx.doi.org/10.1155/2013/681304

17. University of Maryland Medical Center. http://umm.edu/health/medical/altmed/herb/lavender

18. Koulivand, P. H., Ghadiri, M. K., & Gorji, A. (2013). Lavender and the nervous system. *Evidence-Based Complementary and Alternative Medicine.* http://dx.doi.org/ 10.1155/2013/681304

19. Feldman, G., Greeson, J., & Senville, J. (2010). Differential effects of mindful breathing, progressive muscle relaxation, and loving kindness meditation on decentering and negative reactions to repetitive thoughts. *Behavior, Research and Therapy, October: 48) 10); 1002–1011.* doi: 10.1016/j.brat.2010.06.006. Epub 2010 Jun 23.

20. Cappo, B. M., & Holmes, D. S. (1984). The utility of prolonged respiratory exhalation for reducing physiological arousal in non-threatening and threatening situations. *Journal of Psychosomatic Research.* 28 (4), 265–273.

21. Brown, R. P., & Gerbarg, P. L. (2010). Yoga breathing, meditation, and longevity. *Annals Academy of Science August: 1172,* 54–62. doi: 10.1111/j.1749-6632.2009.04394.x

22. Brown, R. P., & Gerbarg, P. L. (2010). Yoga breathing, meditation, and longevity. *Annals Academy of Science August: 1172,* 54–62. doi: 10.1111/j.1749-6632.2009.04394.x

23. Epel, E., Daubenmier, J., Tedlie-Moskowitz, J. Folkman, S., & Blackburn, E. (2009). Can Meditation slow rate of cellular aging? Congitive stress, mindfulness and telomeres. *Ann. N.Y . Academy of Science, 1172,.* 45.

24. Blackburn, E. H., & Epel, E. S. (2013) Too toxic to ignore *Nature; 490,* 169–171.

25. Woodyard, C. (2011). Exploring the therapeutic effects of yoga and its ability to increase quality of life. *International Journal of Yoga. July-December 4 (2),* 49–54.

26. Lasater, J. (1997). The heart of Pantajali, *Yoga Journal 1997: 137,* 134–144.

27. Lasater, J. (1997). The heart of Pantajali, *Yoga Journal 1997: 137,* 134–144.

28. Manjunath, N.K., & Telles, S. (2005). Influence of yoga and ayurveda on self-rated sleep in a geriatric population. *Indian Journal of Medical Research, 2005, 121,* 623–90.

29. Sarang, P., & Telles, S. (2006). Effects of two yoga based relaxation techniques on heart rate variability (HRV) *International Journal of Stress Management, 13 (4) 460–475,* 113.

30. Ross, A. & Thomas, S. (2010). The health benefits of yoga and exercise: A review of comparison Studies. *The Journal of alternative and Complementary Medicine 16,* 3–12.

31. Sleep Deprivation and Deficiency. *National Heart, Lung, and Blood Institute.* https:// www.nhlbi.nih.gov/health/health-topics/topics/sdd/why#

32. Milner, C. E., & Cote, K. A. (2008). A dose-response investigating of the benefits of napping in healthy young, middle aged and older adults. *Sleep and Biological Rhythms. 6,* 2–15.

33. Hayashi, M., Motoyoshi, N., & Hori, T. (2005). Recuperative power of a short daytime nap with or without stage 2 sleep. *Sleep. 28 (7),* 829–836.

34. Tietzel, A. J., & Lack, L. C. (2001). The short-term benefits of brief and long naps following nocturnal sleep restriction. *Sleep 24 (3),* 293–300.

35. Devine, J. K., & Wolf, J. M. (2016). Integrating nap and night-time sleep into sleep patterns reveals differential links to health-relevant outcomes. *Journal of Sleep Research 25,* 225–233.

36. Milner, C. E., & Cote, K. (2009). Benefits of napping in healthy adults: impact of nap length, time of day, age, and experience with napping. *Journal of Sleep Research, 18 (2) June,* 272–281.

37. American Academy of Sleep medicine. Setting standards and promotion excellence in sleep medicine. http://www.aasmnet.org/articles.aspx?id=659

38. Cappuccio, F. P., D'ella, Strazzulo, P., & Miller, M. (2010). Sleep duration and all-cause mortality: A systematic Review and meta-analysis of prospective studies. *Sleep 33 (5)*, 585–592.

39. Harvard Health Publications, Harvard Women's Health Watch Press Release. (2006). *The importance of sleep and health*. www.health.harvard.edu.

40. Rechtschaffen, A., & Bergmann, B. M. (2002). Sleep Deprivation in the rat: An update of the 1989 Paper. *Sleep*. *25*, 18–24.

41. Division of Sleep Medicine: Harvard School and WGBH Educational Foundation. (2008). *Healthy sleep: Sleep and disease risk*. http://healthysleep.med.harvard.edu/healthy/matters/consequences/sleep-and-disease-risk

42. Haravey, A. G., Stinson, K., Whitaker, L., Moskovitz, D., & Virk, H. (2008). The Subjective meaning of sleep quality: A Comparison of individuals with and without insomnia. *Sleep, 31 (3)*, 383–393.

43. Ikeda, H., Kubo, T., Kuriyama, K., & Takahashi, M. (2014). Self-awakening improves alertness in the morning and during the day after partial sleep deprivation. *Journal of Sleep Research (2014), 23*, 673–680.

44. Guadagni, V., Burles, F., Ferrara, M., & Airia, G. (2014). The effects of sleep deprivation on emotional empathy. *Journal of Sleep Research, 23*, 657–663.

45. Takhasi, M. (2012). Prioritizing sleep for healthy work schedules. *Journal of Physiological Anthropology. 3*, 6.

46. National Sleep Foundation. Why is Sleep Important? http://www.resmed.com/us/en/consumer/diagnosis-and-treatment/healthy-sleep/what-hapopens-during-sleep.html)

47. National Heart, Lung and Blood Institute. Sleep Deprivation and Deficiency. https://www.nhlbi.nih.gov/health/health-topics/topics/sdd/why#

48. What makes a good night's sleep, National sleep Foundation. (https://sleepfoundation.org/heathy-sleep-tips

CHAPTER 5

BUILDING HARMONIOUS RELATIONSHIPS

© Maria Napoli

Photo courtesy of Marie Napoli

Open your heart everywhere you go.
Send love to everyone you encounter
then send it back to yourself.

(Napoli)

LEARN TO BUILD
HARMONIOUS RELATIONSHIPS

- Promote positive family, intimate, and work relationships
- Recognize the impact of the Internet on relationships
- Acknowledge the parts of yourself needing development
- Sustain healthy emotional intelligence
- Practice forgiveness and gratitude
- Use the Mindful MAC Guide in all relationships

Feeling the touch of a gentle hand and a warm embrace, experiencing unconditional love and knowing there is someone to share dreams and sorrows all create the bond of a human relationship. Hopefully, one that brings harmony into your life. Relationships are the food that nourishes your emotional, physical, and spiritual selves. Much of your daily thoughts, activities, and conversations are focused on the relationships you have or wish you had. With all the energy and desire people place on their relationships, why are so many unhappy? We yearn to be connected, yet maintaining harmonious relationships is often a challenge. The need to be connected to significant others begins at birth and is the first ingredient to forming a healthy emotional attachment.

Let's take a look at early experiences and how they set the stage for developing personalities and forming relationships. Later in the chapter, key traits that contribute to relationship satisfaction are discussed.

PRIMARY AND DISOWNED SELF

Danilo Sanino/Shutterstock.com

Hal and Sidra Stone's concept of the *primary and disowned self* is a simple model that describes how you develop patterns of emotions, thoughts, and behaviors that define you. You develop your primary self during your growing years when you identify yourself with *experiences and values* that were accepted by your families and caregivers. These patterns of thinking and feeling are the cornerstones of your *primary self;* the person you are familiar with and show to the world. An example of primary self would be if you were raised in a home that expected you to accept adult opinions regardless if you disagreed you learned to hold back your "voice" as an adult. Behaviors that enforce the primary self might be "saying yes when you mean no to avoid conflict" or "repressing your opinion and not say anything."

In contrast, parts of you that were *rejected* in the growing-up process are your disowned selves. These are emotions, thoughts, and behaviors that have not been nurtured, yet are still very much an important part of who you are. An example of your disowned self would be if you were raised in an environment where you experienced lack of praise for accomplishments. You may then choose relationships with people who are egocentric or boast about themselves. In so doing, you gain satisfaction by watching others "pat themselves on the back" instead of acknowledging your own accomplishments.

Both your primary and disowned selves make up your personality and dictate how you behave in relationships. Acknowledging and developing your disowned self releases you from being stuck in the negative dance of expectations that never seems to end. We repeat old patterns with our children, friends, and family for generations when our disowned selves are hidden; thus, happiness eludes us.

As you develop, your primary self, the self you feel most familiar and comfortable with, has been nurtured for better or worse. Since your disowned self is that part of you that did not receive acceptance, you may seek out that part of yourself in your partners, children, employers, co-workers, and friends. "We search out others to satisfy those parts of ourselves that we have disowned and rejected by expecting others to meet those needs."[1] In fact, we often choose partners who mirror those parts of ourselves we reject. Take a moment and reflect upon the characteristics that define your *primary self* and those that define your *disowned self*. Think about how these become visible in your relationships.

PRIMARY SELF CHARACTERISTICS	DISOWNED SELF CHARACTERISTICS

WHERE WE BEGIN

People begin to develop their primary selves from the moment they are born. All experiences from that point on help determine the adult you become. *Infants* thrive on being soothed when in pain, want to be held for safety and comfort, and seek out consistent nurturing from the familiarity of caregivers. Infants form attachments as a result of the love they receive from their caregivers during rocking, from hugs, coos, and smiles received. These experiences are transformed by the infant's sensory systems into patterned neuronal activity that influences the development of the brain in positive ways helping infants to grow and survive.[2] When babies feel nurtured in their relationships, they readily learn to become interdependent with others. For example, babies may reach out to a parent and give them their toy or offer to share their food.

Anneka/Shutterstock.com

They readily smile, hug, and soothe distressed parents by stroking their faces or offering a kiss. This is the beginning of developing empathy, a core ingredient in healthy relationships. Even at this early stage of growing, infants are forming their primary self, learning how to receive love and acceptance.

It is not unusual to find a big burly dad rolling on the floor, laughing heartily with his toddler, only to go back into a silent shell when connecting with his partner or friends. Lives can be richer if you sustain that magic and sense of vulnerability in all of your experiences. When you allow vulnerability to be seen you open the doors for intimacy and empathy in relationships; the road to happiness. Imagine how fulfilling life could be!

Monkey Business Images/ Shutterstock.com

MOVING TOWARD INDEPENDENCE

Relationships during *adolescence* are a crucial time and a stepping-stone to adulthood. This is when teens step out of their comfort zone and begin to explore the development of closer relationships with friends and romantic relationships. Reflecting upon oneself is also one of the developmental milestones of adolescence. A teen may become self-critical, try on new images, and move back and forth between feelings of euphoria and sadness. Too often parents worry about the negative impact of romantic relationships with adolescents, which may include risky sexual activity and abusive behaviors. When adolescents engage in healthy romantic relationships it can have a positive impact on a) identity, helping gain a clearer understanding of who they are and what they value, b) interpersonal skills through effective communication, negotiating boundaries, developing empathy and emotional resiliency, and coping skills during break ups, and c) emotional support received from those other than parents.[3] Helping adolescents process feelings and express the nuances of their experiences in their relationships with their friends and adults without the fear of judgment can lead to healthier decision making. When parents, friends, and teachers accept and respect the ups and downs of adolescent relationships by responding without reacting or judging they are able to model empathy. Acknowledging adolescents with their drama, emotions, and behaviors will help promote open healthy relationships as they mature into adulthood.

Kzenon/Shutterstock.com

CAREER AND LIFE DECISIONS

Young adults and college age students, like adolescents, often have ideals pertaining to relationships. Results from a study found that 62% of undergraduate students involved in a relationship believed that "all problems can be solved if there is enough love." In this same study, male and female students believed in "love at first sight" and "love conquers all."[4]

Students in university settings often seek help with love relationships as these may interfere with their academic success and retention. For some, this may be the first time they are away from the guidance of their families. As a result, they are left to navigate their way in the world of relationships, making new friends, having the freedom to engage in sexual activity, figuring out ways to manage time for academic study and employment, and feeling the pressure of knowing they singly hold their future in their hands.

All too often, young adults enter the world emotionally ill equipped to handle the plethora of experiences and decisions they need to make. If young adults are lacking the emotional ammunition to engage successfully, they can be helped along the way. Offering courses in life skills to develop harmony and happiness and building healthy relationships beginning in elementary school and continuing through college may be as important as academic curriculum. After all, the wisdom gained from experience, often from relationships encountered, is a key ingredient in building a harmonious life.

I'M HERE, NOW WHAT?

Adults continue to long for connection. People need each other, yet often excessive demands are placed on relationships that can suck the joy out of them. Parents want to dictate a child's life; friends make unrealistic demands, and partners fear rejection and can lose the wonder of intimacy in their relationships. Regardless of whom you are in relationships with, there is one steadfast common factor: you are the main player in all of your relationships. All people want to be happy, yet often they cannot find the tools needed to achieve harmony.

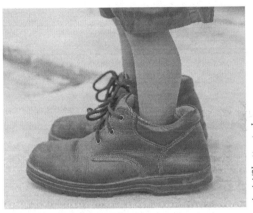

ninsiri/Shutterstock.com

Often people load their relationships with expectations, demands, misperceptions, fear of intimacy, and projections. These frequently lead to conflict and anxiety, and disconnection; the very opposite of what is desired. A sense of self-satisfaction impacts feelings in relationships with others. This is a key element in sustaining satisfying relationships. Reflecting back on the previous discussion of development of the self, it becomes clear that adults who judge their own experiences will undoubtedly place unrealistic demands on their relationships with others. Researchers continue to ask couples what works to maintain satisfaction guidance.

SIX BEHAVIORS IMPORTANT TO RELATIONSHIP SATISFACTION[5]					
1.	2.	3.	4.	5.	6.
Acknowledging the partner	Engaging the partner in every day conversations	Communicating ego building comments such as praising	Exchanging memories about time spent together	Sharing mutual activities	Giving feedback, being mutually honest, and providing encouragement and correction

A feeling of being connected and acceptance of the other is a theme found in relationship satisfaction.[6] Couples who are mindful and mentally engaged are open to new experiences. As mindful individuals, they are less threatened by change, are aware of new contexts, and enjoy more satisfying relationships.[7] Sometimes people need guidance to look at their relationships from a new perspective. Many are fixed in particular ways of behaving, feeling, and thinking. They want to maintain the comfort of sustaining their primary self and are fearful of exploring their disowned self. How often have you heard, "I can't believe I'm doing the same thing as my mother or father!"

The Relationship Enhancement System that follows is a model that focuses on effective communication. It shows ways to help navigate away from patterns of communicating that do not work and develop new healthier ways of communicating that nourish relationships.

RELATIONSHIPS ENHANCEMENT SYSTEM[8]	
Expressive (Owning skill)	One is aware of and owns their feelings
Empathic responding (Receptive Skill)	One listens and gains an understanding of the other person's feelings and motives
Conversive (Discussion-Negotiation/Engagement Skill)	One learns to listen and give back a sense of understanding the meaning of what was heard

Even if you have developed skills for maintaining healthy relationships, you will always need to handle the challenges that face you so that you can keep your balance and harmony.

Rawpixel.com/Shutterstock.com

FRIENDSHIP

Take a moment and reflect upon your *friendships*. Do you feel nourished or depleted in your friendships? You may often reflect upon the significant impact a friend has or has had in your life. Friendships are one of the first relationships you develop away from your family that offer you new opportunities to explore yourself, often without expectations. Women spend a great deal of time conversing with one another sharing feelings and life events. When one is able to connect emotionally with a friend, a feeling of relief, support, and being cared for can improve well-being. It is a known fact that women live longer than men. The reason may be that women connecting with each other are one of the best buffers toward preventing illness. Men have a different way of approaching relationships with their friends. Their "conversations often deal with the doing of things rather than the feelings of things."[9] Regardless of how men and women interact and gain support from each other, the fact remains that friendships are often the backbone of emotional satisfaction for both.

STILL ENJOYING THE RIDE

As *older adults* the need for love and connection does not diminish. Unfortunately, in our western world the media depicts older adults as frail and ill. The fact is older adults have wisdom to share, like to play, enjoy engaging in conversation with others, and desire intimacy. Changing the attitudes of young and middle aged adults toward older adults is necessary so that the expression of sexuality and desire for intimacy and engaging in an active lifestyle is viewed as important. Society holds a cultural belief that restricts the most basic needs of older adults and "this cultural ambivalence, then, seems to be interfering with the physical, psychological and material well-being of older adults."[10] Today people are living longer and have resources to stay healthy as they age. Diffusing the myths of aging increases opportunities for older adults to be viewed as productive and active. The wisdom and life experience of older adults can be life transforming for children, youth, young adults, and adults who are trying to find their way in life.

Elena Ray/Shutterstock.com

WORK RELATIONSHIPS

Many adults spend much of their waking hours working. In addition to job satisfaction and earning a living, it is equally important to have harmonious work relationships. Getting along with co-workers and supervisors will make all the difference in the amount of satisfaction you can achieve at work. When people are at work they engage with others of different age groups, creating different styles of communicating and work ethics. Studies on Millennials (birth years from early 1980s to early 2000s) found that "they work well in teams, are motivated to have an impact on their organizations, favor open and frequent communication with their supervisors and are at ease with communication technologies."[11] Although Millennials thrive on communication in the workplace with supervisors and colleagues, it is important to note that with increased communication comes the responsibility for the knowledge gained. This can be challenging as expectations to do more may not be what Millennials had in mind. The ability and ease of working in groups is critical where diverse opinions and ideas can more readily bring solutions to problems. The comfort level that Millenials have working in teams can be a great asset to the organization and in work relationships. When employees work harmoniously together in teams, work relationships can deepen by team members getting to know one another and creating more opportunities to socialize in and out of the work place.

Monkey Business Images/ Shutterstock.com

Conversely, workers from other generations have been found to have unique characterics that add to the mix of work relationshps. For example, Baby Boomers (birth years from the mid 1940s to the early 1960s) have been found to be ambitious workalcoholics and Generation X workers (birth years from early 1960s to the early 1980s) are skeptical and like to work autonomously; they are less likely to pursue work in groups.[12]

Each generation has something to offer that adds to harmonious work relationships, contribute to work, and organization satisfaction. The following are seven characteristics that build successful work relationships.

SEVEN CHARACTERISTICS OF SUCCESSFUL WORK RELATIONSHIPS[13]	
CHARACTERISTIC	**BEHAVIOR**
Trust	Allow others to do their jobs without unnecessary oversight
Diversity	Learn from differences and broaden solutions
Mindfulness	Encourage expression of new ideas without fear of ridicule or criticism and look for ways to continually learn and improve
Interrelatedness	Be sensitive to tasks at hand and understand how their work affects one another
Respect	Have interactions that are considerate, honest, and tactful. Value others' opinions and are willing change their minds in response to what others say
Varied Interaction	Experience work relationships that are social as well as task oriented. Both are encouraged and add to work relationship satisfaction
Effective Communication	Find a balance between face-to-face interactions, which are rich, as well as interactions such as emails or memos

It is sometimes difficult to be authentic in the workplace, particularly when your livelihood is dependent upon how you are perceived by others. It can be stressful, yet it is important that you remain true to yourself. You might ask yourself the question "Am I employed in a healthy work environment?" Check to see! A healthy work environment has been identified as having four key ingredients:

1. Treats employees with respect and fairness
2. Practices trust between management and employees
3. Supports communication and collaboration. Views each person as valuable in decisions about how they impact the workers as well as how they bring financial gain to the organization
4. Creates an environment where employees feel physically and emotionally safe[14]

Think about where you work. Does the organization create a healthy work environment, opening doors for workers to have harmonious relationships? Regardless of where you work, learning how to effectively communicate with co-workers and supervisors is an essential skill. Five skills have been identified on how YOU can create a healthy work environment.[15]

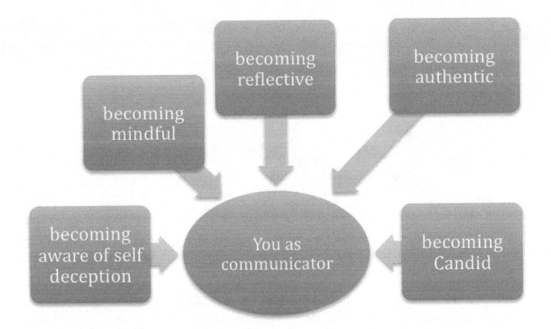

For the better part of your life you will be spending a great deal of time at work and many of your long term relationships will be formed in the organizations in which you work. Decades ago, earning a living was the most important aspect of working. Yet today, it has been found that the working environment and the relationships people have impact not only career opportunities or lack of them, but all aspects of life: health, happiness, physical, and emotional safety. Mindfully, being aware of and responding to behaviors that create a healthy work environment and harmonious work relationships is worth the time spent.

VIRTUAL REALITY OR FACE-TO -FACE...FINDING A BALANCE

How has the Internet impacted the nature of relationships? Much of the modern world today is connected in some way to social media: Facebook, smartphone, YouTube, Twitter, blogs, LinkedIn, Snapchat or some other medium. From childhood through older adulthood people now use the Internet to engage with family and friends. You might not be surprised to know that a recent study of classroom students found that two thirds reported using electronic media in class; studying or doing homework.[16] Probably the most used medium for relationship connection is Facebook. College students who use Facebook can improve well-being as they con-

"I used to text, but now there's a patch that allows me to communicate face to face."

Cartoonstock.com

nect with their friends and participate in college life.[17] A study of college students using Facebook found that 81% logged into Facebook daily. The results showed the following:

COLLEGE STUDENTS USING FACEBOOK[18]	
Majority	Has between 200–350 friends, yet the largest number of students maintain relationships with people they already know
Large number	Go to Facebook to pass time when bored, when they receive an email on a wall posting, or for entertainment
Small Number	Use Facebook to develop new relationships or to meet new people
Anxious and fearful	Use Facebook more often to pass the time and to feel less lonely yet those students tend to have fewer Facebook friends

As discussed earlier, your ability to be vulnerable and self disclose is key in forming and maintaining relationships. It is not surprising that if a person is anxious and fearful, he or she may spend more time on Facebook than communicating face to face. Those who have a lot of friends on Facebook use the site to maintain those relationships.

How does Facebook influence couples at various stages in their relationship? Do couples use Facebook more as their relationship progresses? Is the comfort level of going on Facebook the same as the relationship becomes closer and more intimate? It was found that there is a connection between the stage of the relationship and surveillance of Facebook use. Furthermore, as self-disclosure increases, surveillance also increases checking how often a partner is on Facebook. It is not surprising that when couples are getting closer, more intimate and spend more time together, they are more concerned about how much time is spent connecting with people outside of the relationship; maybe to ensure and protect the stability of the relationship. Hence, as the relationship matures, Facebook usage decreases and couples spend more time together building their relationship. On a negative note, regardless of the stage of the relationship, the usage of Facebook was a predictor of jealousy. As the use of Facebook increased, the level of jealousy increased.[19] Trying to integrate various outside relationships into an intimate relationship is a challenge making Facebook a platform to increase jealousy when the couple is trying to learn about each other and grow together as a couple. Although having access to friends and family on Facebook for updates in one's life and sharing information, social media cannot replace the benefits of interacting face to face. Some may think that since the use of social media has increased more people are addicted to Internet use. Although college students are heavy Internet users, research found they do not have withdrawal feelings as someone might have with addictive tendencies when they are not on the internet. As a result, college students, in general, do not have problems with Internet dependence.[20]

Marcos Mesa Sam Wordley/Shutterstock.com

Cartoonstock.com

Has the Internet impacted those in committed relationships in a positive or negative way? A study of couples in committed relationships found they were impacted by Internet use in different ways.

IMPACT OF INTERNET ON COMMITTED PARTNER RELATIONSHIPS[21]	
45% of 18–29 year old couples surveyed	21% reported the Internet had a major impact 24% a minor impact on the relationship
11% of couples 65 and older	1% reported a major impact
41% of 18–29 year old	Felt closer to their partners using online or text conversations and 23% resolved an argument digitally that was difficult to resolve in person
21% of Internet users	Internet use or cell phone owners in committed relationships felt closer to their partners due to exchanges or conversations they had texting
9% of Internet users	Reported resolving an argument online or texting when resolving the problem was difficult to do in person

Life is about finding a balance and Internet use can be beneficial when used responsibly. It is essential to pay attention to how, how much, and whether the time spent on the Internet is interfering with your relationship.

WE ARE ONLY HUMAN

Human beings regardless of age have the same basic needs. Emotional security and companionship have been found to be core elements to happiness in relationships.[22] Surprisingly, it has been found that income has little to do with achieving happiness in relationships[23] and "people with stronger materialistic values have been found to have more negative emotions and less relatedness, autonomy, competence, gratitude, and meaning in life."[24] When people are grateful they spend less time striving for things materialistic and more time leading a meaningful life and cultivating quality relationships.[25] Some people find themselves in a "rut," engaging in the same activities day after day with no change. This can also affect happiness. People who are more curious were found to have more frequent growth-oriented behaviors, and search for meaning and life satisfaction.[26] People need to find personal joy, which may positively impact their relationships. When people are happy they are more motivated to engage in kindness toward others.[27] It's a win-win relationship when you are happy with yourself since you will have a better chance of choosing relationships that are more rewarding. When people are courageous enough to openly self-reflect and share those reflections with another, only then can they truly experience a deep relationship and empathically step into another's shoes. Sharing a deep sense of intimacy is the backbone of a healthy relationship.

What is intimacy? Being comfortable with vulnerability describes intimacy in a nutshell. Intimacy is being in touch with the reality of another person and having a shared internal awareness.[28] In order to be comfortable with vulnerability, you will need to let go of fear of rejection, approval seeking, and expectations. Once you accept yourself, you can swim gracefully into self-disclosing to the important people in your life. Self-disclosure is at the core of experiencing intimacy. Intimate communication is a dance where both parties are engaged and connecting on various levels, verbal, non-verbal, experiencing each other through sensory stimuli. As discussed earlier, as you become comfortable with your vulnerability, and exploring your disowned self, you open more opportunities for balance within yourself and harmony in your relationships.

"KNOW WHAT, MOM? WITH ALL YOUR FAULTS I STILL LOVE YA!"

MASTERING THE GOODS

It is important to know where you have been, to carve out the path to where you are going. How people develop and how the experiences encountered impact who they become has been discussed. In fact, how early attachments develop your primary and disowned self-personality is not new knowledge. Psychology literature over the last century has identified the importance of the relationship between caregivers and healthy emotional development significantly contributing to lasting relationship satisfaction. "Children who are strongly attached to their parents and have little conflict with them are more likely than others to be happy in marriage when they become men and women.[29] To add to your life experiences, let's look at some key traits that can foster harmony in your relationships. It is important to note that harmony does not mean that one is happy or feeling positive all the time. You need to have the ability to resolve conflict, which is one building block to strengthen your relationships through the lessons you learn from working through challenges. Sometimes one method of resolving conflict may actually create conflict at another time or for different relationships. When you let go of judgments and expectations you are better able to make decisions about how you can respond to situations. "When we are mindful, being present in the moment and open to the experience one may increase the opportunity for having a positive experience."[30]

Forgiveness and gratitude are two of the best tools for sustaining harmony. Much of the literature on healthy relationships has focused on conflict resolution. Yet, it has been suggested that studying the characteristics of what constitutes a healthy relationship is important[31] because it is important to understand the causes of dysfunction and conflict as well as study tools that lead to relationship satisfaction.[32] When people are mindful they are able to acknowledge experiences without filters increasing the opportunity for trust and intimacy in their relationships.

"I received your text message about the importance of tolerance and forgiveness. Now what did you do?"

RELIEF OF LETTING GO

In chapter one, the importance of self-forgiveness was discussed and how it increases self-esteem. When people are able to forgive wrongdoings of others, they not only open the doors for a healthier relationship, but they also relieve themselves from carrying pain, anger, and resentment. When you are able to forgive, you are more likely to self-regulate with the goal of improving a relationship and inhibiting the tendency to damage the relationship by using negative interpersonal tactics such as hitting, berating, or avoiding.[33] Mindfully letting go of feelings you have toward others can be relieving and refreshing, creating space for transformation and growth. Another aspect of forgiveness is the ability to regulate negative feelings. When you can respond instead of react to others who you feel wronged you, the parasympathetic system of the brain is more likely to be stimulated. This system activates healing and relaxation instead of the sympathetic system that activates the fight or flight response. When you forgive, the benefits are mutual.

THE ULTIMATE GIFT

There is no mystery about the power gratitude can have on your life. Recently there has been a plethora of research describing the benefits of gratitude. Gratitude has been found to increase relationship satisfaction, facilitate socially inclusive behaviors, and promote social affiliation.[34] Gratitude has been found to increase the perception of the strength of relationships when expressing gratitude to a relationship partner and gratitude to a friend.[35] Expressing gratitude was found to increase comfort in being able to voice concerns in a relationship. In addition those who expressed gratitude had a more positive perception of their partner than those who did not express gratitude.[36] A key point in expressing gratitude is knowing that the person you are expressing gratitude to perceives the gesture as what you intended. Here again, when you are mindful you do not make assumptions, but are present for your experiences and pay attention to the interactions you are having with others by noticing emotions, body language, senses, and instincts. Research has found that those who perceived expression of gratitude from the expresser were more likely to have better relationship outcomes.[37] Your ability to communicate your intentions and pay attention to the person's response, both verbal and non-verbal, is important.

Taking what was discussed in this chapter, how do you sustain the magic in your relationships? Can you accept the unpredictability of them, their autonomy, and their mystery? Can you accept the uniqueness in each of your relationships? How wonderful it is that you can have the ability to unglue yourself from your past and unleash your disowned, unconscious self.

You now have the ingredients and tools to embrace and experience harmonious relationships. These can provide you with many opportunities to live a life with others filled with enchantment and awe.

MINDFULNESS PRACTICE
USING THE MINDFUL MAC GUIDE

Mindful MAC Guide

acknowledge
attention
accept
choose

1. Mindfully **acknowledge** each experience without internal or external filters

2. Intentionally pay **attention** to your senses, thoughts, emotions, and instincts regarding each experience

3. **Accept** your experience without judgment or expectations

4. **Choose** to respond versus react to your experience

Discuss how well you did with your practice this week, feelings you had, obstacles you faced and how you overcame them.

_____

_____

_____

_____

_____

_____

_____

_____

_____

_____

_____

_____

_____

_____

_____

_____

_____

_____

_____

_____

_____

DESIGNER ACTIVITIES

Please answer the following:

1. Who are the important people in my life?

_____

_____

_____

2. What expectations have I placed on my relationships?

_____

_____

_____

3. I have difficulty listening empathically when:

_____

_____

_____

Disowned Self- the part of you that is hidden and needs visibility

1. Make a list of the characteristics that describe you.

2. Make another list of the characteristics that describe the significant people in your life.

Characteristics of Self   **Characteristics of significant others**

_____

_____

_____

What are you aware of now?

_____

_____

_____

Significant Mindful Relationships

Activity #1—Though my child's eyes

- Choose a week for simply noticing your child
- During all of your interactions with your child see the world from his/her eyes
- Take a moment to reflect on how you feel about being in your child's shoes
- Notice what it feels like to have you as a parent.

Activity #2—An offering of myself

- Choose a week to simply notice a person you are living with
- Every day spend an hour in an activity together
- Listen without interrupting during the entire interaction
- Notice how the interaction is different
- Pay attention to that person's body, behavior, thoughts, and interactions
- Pay attention to your body, behaviors, thoughts, and interactions

Friend Connection

Activity #1

- Find a quiet place
- Bring the image of a friend into focus
- Think about times spent together
- Create an opportunity to spend time with that friend

Activity #2

- Find a quiet place
- Bring the image of a friend into focus
- Make an offering of your heart to your friend
- Share your offering with your friend

Harmonious Relationships in My Life

Think of the people with whom you share your life. In the diagram, place the name of someone important to you in the larger center circle and identify the significant characteristics that make up that relationship in the smaller circles. Add more circles if necessary.

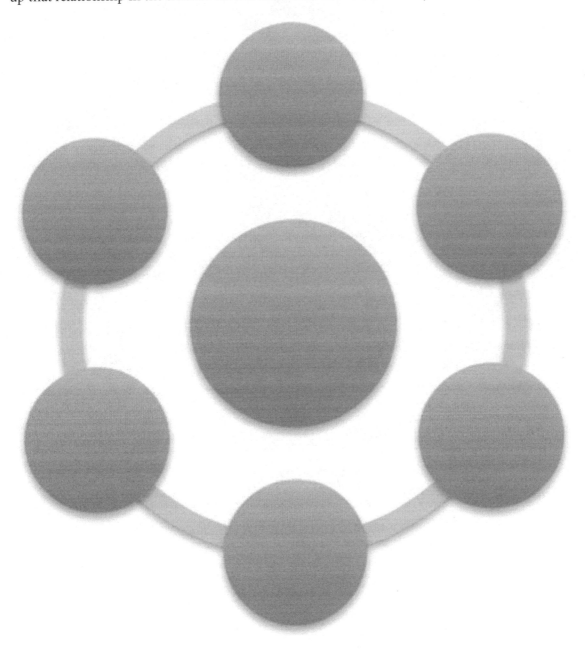

In this next diagram, Place the name of that same person in the larger center circle and identify what characteristics you would like to see or what you would like to say to that person in the smaller circles. Add more circles if necessary.

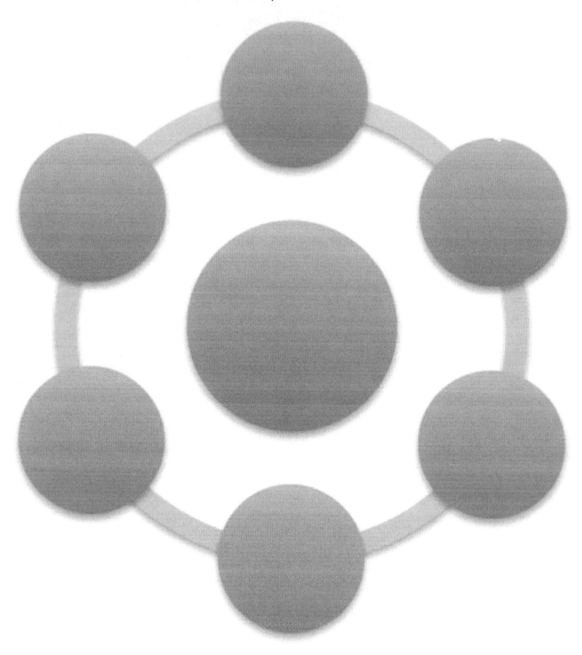

Internet Activity

Explore how much time you spend on the Internet and evaluate if you might want to be spending more time engaging with others face to face.

ACTIVITY	HOW TIME IS SPENT	HOW TIME COULD BE SPENT
Texting		
Email		
Facebook		
Internet surfing		
Tweeting		
Blogging		

Forgiveness

Find a quiet place to sit or lie down. Reflect upon a time when you felt wronged by someone you cared about. Let that person know how their behavior made you feel. Send forgiveness to that person. Take a breath, note how you feel. Describe the situation before and after forgiveness

_____

_____

_____

Gratitude

1. Find a comfortable seated position. Close your eyes. Allow your body to be held by the chair. Notice the bodily sensation of contact with the chair.
2. Relax your abdomen. Notice that your breath is already moving on its own. Follow the breath for a few moments.
3. Bring to mind a visual image or a felt sense of someone who embodied the quality of loving-kindness. Imagine that this person is sitting across from you.
4. Now imagine that you are emanating feelings of gratitude toward that person.
5. When your attention wanders, simply return to this image or felt sense of the person and begin again.

LIFE BY PERSONAL DESIGN
REFLECTIVE JOURNAL

In this Reflective Journal, record what you learned from this chapter, your "intentions" for change, any barriers you think might interfere with these desired changes and how you will overcome them, and at least *one* strategy that will help you realizeyour dreams and the life you will love.

_____

_____

_____

_____

_____

_____

_____

_____

_____

_____

_____

_____

_____

_____

_____

_____

_____

_____

_____

_____

_____

_____

_____

_____

READINGS OF INTEREST

Abowitz, D. A., Knox, D., Zusman, M., & McNeely, A. (2009). Beliefs about romantic relationships: gender differences among undergraduates. *College Student Journal, June.*

Barber, B., & Eccles, J. (2003). The joy of romance: Healthy adolescent relationships as an educational agenda. In P. Florsheim (Ed). *Adolescent romantic relationships and sexual behavior: Theory, research and practical implications.* Mahwah, NJ: Lawrence Eribaum Associates.

Christakis, N. A, & Fowler, J. H. (2007). The spread of obesity in a large social network over 32 years. *The New England Journal of Medicine 357 July,* 370–379.

Kasha, T. B., & Breen, W. E. (2007). Materialism and diminished well being: Experiential avoidance as a mediating mechanism. *Journal of Social and Clinical Psychology May 26 (5),* 521–539.

Moore, T. (1994). *Soul Mates: Honoring the mysteries of love and relationship.* NY: Harper Perennial.

Zaslow, J. (2010, April). Friendship for guys (No tears!). *The Wall Street Journal.*

REFERENCES

1. Stone H., & Stone S. (2007). The psychology of selves in embracing each other. Chapter 1 *Voice Dialogue International* (http://delos-inc.com/Reading_Room/Book_Chapters/EEO/eeo.html

2. Perry, B. D. (2001). Attachment: The first core strength. *Early Childhood Today, October.*

3. Sorensen, S. (2007). Adolescent romantic relationships. *ACT for Youth Center of Excellence Research Facts and Findings, July.*

4. Know, D., Schacht, C., & Zusman, M. E. (1999). Love relationships among college students. *College Student Journal, March.*

5. Schumway, S. T., & Wampler, R.,S. (2002). A behaviorally focused measures for relationships: The couple behavior report. *The American Journal of Family Therapy 30,* 311-321.

6. Young, M. A. (2004). Healthy relationships: Where's the research? *The Family Journal: Counseling and Therapy for Couples and Families April. 12 (2),* 159–162.

7. Burpee, C., & Langer, E. J. (2005). Mindfulness and marital satisfaction. *Journal of Adult Development Vol. 12 January,* 43–51.

8. Nichols, M. P., & Schwartz, R. C. (2006). *Family therapy concepts and methods.* Boston: Pearson, 309.

9. Zaslow, J. (2010, April). Friendship for guys (No tears!). *The Wall Street Journal.*

10. Wood-Aleman, M. (2008). Enabling romantic relationships in later life: Discarding cultural myths and facilitation dialogue. *The Oates Journal, October: 12:13,* 1–8.

11. Demir, M. (2008). Sweetheart, you really make me happy: Romantic relationship quality and personality as predictors of happiness among emerging adults. *Journal of Happiness Studies 9,* 257–277.

12. Meyers, K. K., & Sadaghiani, K. (2010). Millennials in the workplace: A communication perspective on Millennials' organizations' relationships and performance. *Journal of Business Psychology 25*, 225–238.

13. Meyers, K. K., & Sadaghiani, K. (2010). Millennial in the workplace: A communication perspective on Millennials' organizations relationships and performance. *Journal of Business Psychology 25*, 225–238.

14. Tallia, A. F., Lanham, H. J.M., McDaniel, R. R., & Crabtree, B. F. (2006). Seven characteristics of successful work relationships. *Family Practice Management January* (13), 47–50.

15. Shirey, M. R. (2006). Authentic leaders creating healthy work environments for nursing practice. *American Journal of Critical Care. May 15 (3)*, 268.

16. Kupperschmidt, B, Kientz, E., Ward, J., & Reinholz, B. (2010). A healthy work environment: It begins with you. *The Online Issues in Nursing 15. Manuscript 3*, 1-9.

17. Jacobsen, W. C., & Forste, R. (2010). The wired generation: Academic and social outcomes of electronic media use among university students. *Cyberpsychology, Behavior, and Social Networking 14 (5)*, 275–80.

18. Kalpidou, M., Costin, D., & Morris, J. (2011). The relationship between Facebook and the well-being of undergraduate college students. *Cyberpsychology, Behavior and Social Networking 14 (4)*, 183–189.

19. Sheldon, P. (2008). The relationship between unwillingness-to-communicate-and students' Facebook use. *Journal of Media Psychology 20 (2)*, 67–75.

20. Farrugia, R. (2013). Facebook and relationships: A study of how social media use is affection long-term relationships *Thesis Rochester Institute of Technology.*

21. Mitchell, K. A., & Beard, F. (2010, Spring). Measuring Internet dependence among college students: A replication and confirmatory analysis. *Southwestern Mass Communication Journal*, 15–28.

22. Lenhart, A., & Duggen. (2014). Couples, the Internet, and social media: How American couples use digital technology to manage life, logistics and emotional intimacy within their relationships. *Pew Research Center, February, Couples, the Internet and Social Media.*

23. Demir, M. (2008). Sweetheart, you really make me happy: Romantic relationship quality and personality as predictors of happiness among emerging adults. *Journal of Happiness Studies 9*, 257–277.

24. North, R. J., Holahan, C. H., Moos, R. H., & Cronkite, R. C. (2008).Family support, family income and happiness: a 10 year perspective. *Journal of Family Psychology 22 (3)*, 475–483.

25. Kashadan, T. B., & Breen, W.E. (2007). Materialism and diminished well being: Experiential avoidance as a mediating mechanism. *Journal of Social and Clinical Psychology May 26 (5)*, 521–539.

26. Polak, E.L., & Mcullough, M. E. (2006). Is gratitude an alternative to materialism? *Journal of Happiness Studies 7*, 343–360.

27. Kashdan, T. B., & Steger, M. F. (2007). Curiosity and pathways to well being and meaning in life: Traits, states, and everyday behaviors. *Motivation and Emotion 31*, 159–173.

28. Otake, K., Simai, S., Tanaka-Matsumi, J., Otsui, K., & Fredrickson, B.L. (2006). happy people become happier through kindness: A counting kindnesses intervention. *Journal of Happiness Studies 7*, 361–375.

29. Mosier, W. (2006, March 22). Intimacy: The key to a healthy relationship. *Annals of the American Psychotherapy Association.*

30. Caughlin, J. P., & Huston, T. L. (2010). The flourishing literature on flourishing relationships. *Journal of Family Theory and Review 2 March*, 25–3.

31. Fincham, F. D., & Beach (2010). Of memes and marriage: Toward a positive relationship science. *Journal of Family Theory and Review, 2* (March), 4–24.

32. Young, M. A. (2004). Healthy relationships: Where's the research? *The Family Journal: Counseling and Therapy for Couples and Families April. 12 (2)*, 159–162.

33. Beach, S. R. H., & Fincham, F. D. (2010). Conflict can be constructive: Reflections on the dialectics of relationship science. *Journal of Family Theory and Review, 2 (March)*, 54–57.

34. Braithwaite, S. R., Selby, E. A., & Fincham, F. D. (2011). Forgiveness and relationship satisfaction: Mediating mechanisms. *Journal of Family Psychology August; 25 (4)* 551–559.

35. Bartlett, M. Y., Cruz, C. P., Bauman, J., & Desteno, D. (2012). Gratitude: Prompting behaviors that build relationships. *Cognition and Emotion 26*, 2–13.

36. Lambert, N. M., Clark, M. S., Durtschi, J., Fincham, F. D., & Graham, S. M. (2010). Benefits of expressing gratitude: Expressing gratitude to a partner changes one's view of the lationship. *Psychological Science April 21 (4)*, 574–580.

37. Lambert, Fincham. (2011). Expressing gratitude to a partner leads to more relationship maintenance behavior. *Emotion, 11*, 52–60.

38. Algoe, S. B., & Zhaoyang, R. (2016). Positive psychology in context: Effects of expressing gratitude in ongoing relationships depend on perceptions of enactor responsiveness. *The Journal of Positive Psychology 11 (4)*, 399–415.

CHAPTER 6

PROTECTING YOUR LIFE SPACE: ENVIRONMENTAL AWARENESS

Photo courtesy of Maria Napoli

© Maria Napoli

Earth is our home
We have nowhere else to go
Everyday remember to cherish
Clean water to cleanse
Clean air to oxygenate
Clean land to nourish
Keep it safe
Keep is beautiful
Our future is now

(Napoli)

- Importance of clean water, air and land
- Sustainable energy
- Essentials for supporting quality life
- Global warming
- Reducing your carbon footprint
- Creating a healthy environment for ourselves and children
- Personal solutions for sustainable living in home, work and community

As you move along in your day, you eat, wash, drink, and breathe. Most likely you take these simple activities for granted. All too often, our over indulgence in today's world has made these basic essentials for healthy living a rare commodity. We are polluting our food, water, and air, all of which contributes to our demise with the increase in preventable illnesses such as cancer, autoimmune deficiency, respiratory illness, and heart disease. Approximately 40% of deaths worldwide are caused by water, air, and soil pollution. The causes are environmental degradation and growth in world population, which contribute to an increase in human disease.[1] The field of environmental medicine is becoming widespread as more people suffer from illnesses due to airborne chemicals in the workplace, community, and home.

Photo courtesy of Maria Napoli

All living things are interdependent upon each other. Plants need carbon dioxide that humans produce, humans need oxygen that plants produce, and animals, birds, fish, and insects provide a balance in our ecology of air, water, and land. To keep yourself alive and well you might look at what your body is made up of: 65% oxygen, 18% carbon, 10% hydrogen, 3% nitrogen, 1.5% calcium, 1% phosphorous, and 1.5% remaining minerals.[2] All of these elements are available in nature and dwindling due to man's greed and reckless violence toward our planet. Ecologists say that it is not too late, yet many people seem oblivious to the problems we are creating that can be prevented if we paid attention to our behavior and began taking action in our own lives.

AIR

There's so much pollution in the air now that if it weren't for our lungs there'd be no place to put it all.

~**Robert Orben**[3]

The leading causes of air pollution are motor vehicle emissions, chemical plants, coal-fired power plants, oil refineries, petrochemical plants, nuclear waste disposal activity, incinerators, and large livestock farms.[4] We can prevent the increase in premature deaths, asthma, and mercury contamination by demanding cleaner power plant regulations. With so many chemicals being introduced, the incidence of multiple chemical sensitivity (MCS) is increasing. Children are at risk as their tissues grow rapidly and their detoxification systems are immature.[5] You cannot control the quality of air in your neighborhoods yet you do have some control in your home. For example, plants provide oxygen, and installing wood or stone floors instead of carpets, changing air filters, and controlling dust in air ducts, fans, draperies and shades and mites in beds can all contribute to cleaner air in your home. Your body is increasingly affected by multiple chemicals in daily living, yet you are often most likely unaware of their detrimental effects.

As an adult you may be aware of the changes in your daily functioning, yet frequently ignore them due to time constraints placing your attention on your routines and the activities that take precedence. For example, you may have a general feeling of un-wellness and visit your physician, yet your doctor cannot find anything wrong. Illness related to chemicals is rapidly becoming a problem, yet we are often at a loss as how to identify and treat diseases related to it. Recently pollution-related illnesses are being studied in the field of environmental medicine. They are beginning to identify what pollution does at the cellular level, the level of biochemistry where energy is produced. Some problems resulting from environmental pollution are:[6]

PROBLEM	SYMPTOMS
Brain fog	Poor concentration
Autoimmunity	Frequent infections (yeast and fungal)
Asthma	Respiratory distress
Emotional instability	Mood swings: anger, frustration
Recurrent muscle strains	Tendons, ligaments
Sleep disorders	Waking between 1–3 AM

When you are exposed to volatile organic compounds (VOCs) such as petro chemicals and other forms of commercial solvent type chemicals, these chemicals are rapidly sponged out of the bloodstream and stored in the fatty tissues of your body. Your brain, like the liver and heart, has a rich blood supply and high fat content; thus, the brain is a primary target for chemicals to hide. By the time these environmental pollutants are recognized it is too late to treat.[7] The following illnesses can be prevented without chemical pollution.

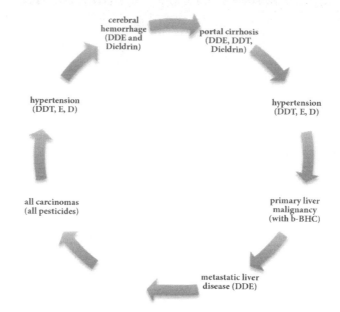

Now that we have looked at some of the problems, let's take a look at some solutions that can improve your physical, mental and aesthetic home environment. Your immune system is able to fight off viruses and bacteria yet is not able to help eliminate or recognize toxic metals in your body. Using an infrared sauna is a simple way to eliminate chemicals from your body. Because the infrared saunas heat penetrates (up to 1¾ inches compared to the traditional sauna, which only penetrates approximately ⅛ of an inch), your body can get a good detoxifying sweat going at about 120 degrees as compared to 180 degrees required from a traditional sauna.

BENEFITS OF AN INFRARED SAUNA

- Causes weight loss (without having to lift a finger)
- Helps treat cellulitis
- Improves your immune system
- Improves your strength and vitality
- Helps cure several skin diseases like eczema, psoriasis, and acne
- Strengthens the cardio-vascular system
- Helps control your blood pressure
- Detoxifies your body
- Gives you more energy and relieves stress
- Helps treat burns and scars
- Relieves pain (joint pain, sore muscles, arthritis)
- Helps control your cholesterol level
- Helps treat bronchitis

[8] http://www.infrared-sauna-reference.com

When your body is given the opportunity to do its job, it has the innate capacity to discharge toxins and store nutrients. Your lungs, liver, kidneys, and skin are the key to your waste elimination. If you give these organs a chance to do their jobs, you are on the road to being pollution free.

KEEP YOUR BODY POLLUTION FREE

How does fiber work to help your body eliminate pollution? If fiber is deficient then waste will be reabsorbed back into your portal vein and lymphatic chain (think immune system). Additionally, if there is an overgrowth of bad bacteria, then they can facilitate re-absorption of cellular waste, pollution, and excess hormones back into your body.[9]

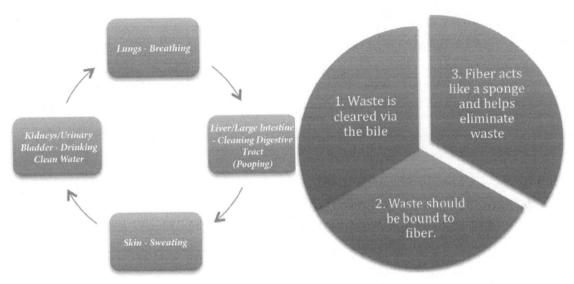

There is hope, and you can make a difference in your personal life, home, work, and community. When you are mindful of what you eat, how you use energy, and protect yourself by using chemical free products, you begin to create the healthy life you deserve.

YOUR HOME

"Organic chemicals are widely used as ingredients in household products. Paints, varnishes, and wax all contain organic solvents, as do many cleaning, disinfecting, cosmetic, degreasing, and hobby products."[10] A study of household dust found that 10 chemicals known or thought to harm humans are found in 90% of household dust such as furniture and toys. Although dust may seem like a harmless pollutant it can make you more vulnerable to respiratory problems and cancer.[11] Walk around your house and notice your surroundings. You may initially take in the decorations, furniture, and artifacts that you have accumulated over the years.

radoma/Shutterstock.com

Now take another walk around your house; this time take a closer look in your cabinet drawers, closets, refrigerator, ceiling fans, pictures, and underneath your sink. You might be surprised at what you find. You might say to yourself, "This place needs a good cleaning." Ok, if this is the case, go to your cleaning supply cabinet and bath and cosmetic products and examine the ingredients that are contained in them. My guess is that most of the ingredients include chemicals that you cannot even pronounce or recognize. If you are cleaning your countertops and table where you eat and prepare food, you are probably ingesting those chemicals. If you are cleaning your floors, you are taking them in through your skin if you walk barefoot. Interesting thoughts?

Have you ever thought about where the shoes and clothes you wear come from and what materials they are made from? The buzz for sustainable apparel is up and coming and the big names are joining the coalition. Beginning with Walmart and Patagonia and now having more than 60 members, the development of the Sustainable Apparel Coalition's goal is to "join together to develop an index to measure the environmental impact of their products." These companies account for more than a third of the global apparel and footwear industry. Measuring the energy use, greenhouse gas emissions, water consumption, chemical use, and waste of their factories around the world are some of the initiatives taking place. The "Clean by Design" organization is a revolutionary company with a mission to engage clothing retailers and suppliers to improve efficiency, decrease environmental impact and reduce waste, water use and energy consumption as well as save money and provide longer lasting clothing. Their 10-step best practice initiative includes everything from the manufacturing process to how people care for their garments. Clean by Design's efforts at more than 50 textile mills in China have resulted in a 400 ton reduction in chemicals, as well as decreases of 36% in water usage and 22% in energy usage per mill. Linda Greer, a senior scientist with the Natural Resources Defense Council said, "the purity of the concept is what makes it such a modern approach to improving the planet."[12]

SOLUTIONS TO PROTECT YOUR HOME

- Make cleaning products from aromatherapy
- Clean more often
- Check labels
- Ask more questions
- Utilize cleaning strategies such as avoiding the use of hot water, diluting each detergent as much as possible, and applying soft no acidic or non-abrasive detergents for a few minutes to reduce exposure to detergents [13]
- Use cosmetics and creams without chemicals
- Choose carpets with natural fibers
- Choose clothing with natural fibers
- Invest in an air purifier
- Buy energy efficient appliances
- Switch to energy efficient light bulbs
- Turn down your hot water thermostat to 60 degrees F
- Arrange furniture with *feng shui* and purchase ecologically friendly materials
- Bring in more air from outdoors
- Safely clean your home

WATER

Photo courtesy of Maria Napoli

The importance of providing your body with clean water cannot be overestimated. Your body can no longer be regenerated by drinking water from the tap or local rivers. Our rivers today are full of chemicals such as lead, aluminum, sodium fluoride, bacteria and viruses, chlorine, chloroform, MTBE-rocket fuel, pesticides, treated and filtered waste water, antibiotics, and antidepressants, to name a few. These pollutants cause fatigue, diminished cellular performance and stunted cellular growth.[14] Illnesses related to polluted drinking water are extensive, such as malaria, hepatitis and other viruses. People die every day from drinking polluted water. The number of people lacking clean water is astounding. It is estimated that 1.2 billion people lack clean water and water born infections account for 80% of all infectious diseases. A shocking Associated Press investigation found various pharmaceuticals in the drinking supplies of at least 41 million Americans. Even extremely diluted concentrations of pharmaceutical residues harm fish, frogs and other aquatic species in the wild, and human cells fail to grow normally when exposed to trace concentrations of certain drugs.[15]

The fact remains that we need to conserve the clean water we have and find ways to prevent polluting this essential commodity that we need to survive.

Take a moment and think about water more consciously.

- Drink bottled water
- Conserve water when taking a shower or brushing your teeth
- Conserve water by using plants indigenous to your environment
- Drink two quarts of water daily to nourish and flush toxins from your body. Drink water from glass, or stainless container (no plastic), and install reverse osmosis if possible

LAND

The foods you eat today often contain chemicals either from the soil they were grown on or preservatives to sustain shelf life. One rule to follow when you are shopping for food is to avoid products that have chemical names that you do not know how to pronounce as well as products with sugar and corn sweeteners. It is astonishing how many products have these additives. Shopping the outer perimeters of the store where fresh foods are usually displayed instead of the middle aisles where canned and boxed foods are shelved may help you make better choices. When you think about food only a century ago, you might visualize foods that were grown by the families who harvested them instead of buying food from a supermarket. It is also likely that those foods were not full of pesticides and those foods supplied vitamins and minerals to help grow healthy cells in the body. The Environmental Protection Agency has approved 350 ingredients for food uses—200 of which account for 98% of the pesticides currently applied to agricultural products many of them polluting water and killing plants and wildlife. "Farm workers who mix, load or apply certain pesticides have contracted serious illnesses and in some cases died from direct exposure, according to health officials."[16]

In order for your body to be healthy, you need to have a greater percentage of alkalinity versus acidity. Remember reading earlier in the chapter what your body is made up of: 65% oxygen, 18% carbon, 10% hydrogen, 3% nitrogen, 1.5% calcium, 1% phosphorous, and 1.5% remaining minerals. Note that oxygen is most important; therefore supplying our bodies with air and foods that give versus deplete oxygen is what we need to focus on. When our bodies are acidic, we are more susceptible to illness as the balance is disrupted. Your body becomes acidic when it is exposed to non-foods such as chemicals, excess fats, and stress. Organic foods are a great way to support alkalinity in your blood stream and within your cells. Organic foods have a higher nutrient density than conventional foods, a higher antioxidant potential, higher enzyme capacity, and higher energy potential and are typically farmed in humane and sustainable ways without environmental pollution and bacterial infections. When you maintain a happy and emotionally balanced life, you support your body's alkalinity. Consuming large amounts of foods and eating foods with preservatives and chemicals contribute to the growing obesity epidemic in children and adults.

Obesity is rapidly becoming one of the most deadly environmental illnesses. Unlike years ago where famine killed thousands of people, today human beings live in the age of obesity, too much food and food that does not nourish the body and often contaminates it. A survey of 360 articles published between January 1989 and April 2009, and 12 major newspapers in the United States, Canada and United Kingdom reported that obesity is a lifestyle problem, yet individuals, governments and industry need to share a role in addressing the modern environments.[17] Your body has amazing innate intelligence. It knows exactly where to send nutrients, through food, vitamins, and minerals ingested by eating and breathing.

A simple daily activity can save your life—hand washing. Why is hand washing so important? Your hands are the main avenue for germ transmission and properly washing your hands can prevent germ transmission. Here are some suggestion when and how to wash your hands.

WHEN SHOULD YOU WASH YOUR HANDS?

- Before, during, and after preparing food
- Before eating food
- Before and after caring for someone who is sick
- Before and after treating a cut or wound
- After using the toilet
- After changing diapers or cleaning up a child who has used the toilet
- After blowing your nose, coughing, or sneezing
- After touching an animal, animal feed, or animal waste
- After handling pet food or pet treats
- After touching garbage

HOW SHOULD YOU WASH YOUR HANDS?

- Wet your hands with clean, running water (warm or cold).
- Turn off the tap and apply soap.
- Lather your hands by rubbing them together with the soap. Be sure to lather the backs of your hands, between your fingers, and under your nails.
- Scrub your hands for at least 20 seconds. Need a timer? Hum the "Happy Birthday" song from beginning to end twice.
- Rinse your hands well under clean, running water.
- Dry your hands using a clean towel or air dry them.[18]

SAVE OUR CHILDREN

Photo courtesy of Maria Napoli

Life has changed dramatically for children today. The days seem long lost when children found complete joy in the fresh air playing outdoors without a thought of video games, smartphones, or television. The more children play indoors, the more their connection to nature dwindles. The media does not help with advertising and parents who are overworked often depend upon the technology of electronics to keep children busy. In addition, the increase in crimes against children may contribute to parents wanting their children to be safe, sacrificing play in nature. "In a typical week, only 6% of children ages nine to thirteen were found to play outside on their own; bike riding is down 31% since 1995; 90% of inner-city children do not know how to swim, and 34% have never been to a beach. Schools have canceled field trips, have buildings with no windows and many have eliminated outdoor or all physical education programs."[19]

The effects of outdoor pollution (OAP) on children's health cannot be underestimated. Children 6–12 years old who are exposed to air pollution related to traffic-dense areas had a higher incidence of respiratory symptoms and asthma. Children who attend school have been at risk for asthma, poor attendance due to adverse health effects, and high levels of CO_2 due to poor air quality and ventilation. The National Poison Data System reported that in children under five years old, the top 10 leading cause of poisonous deaths were analgesics, batteries, hydrocarbons, plants, cold and cough preparations, fumes/gases/vapors, and pesticides, anti-depressants, chemicals, and household cleaning substances.[20] Though technology has bene-fited the cognitive development of children, the problems of living in an industrialized modern society often outweigh the benefits. For example, the need for vitamin D, the sunshine vitamin, is "vital for the formation and maintenance of healthy bones in children, adults and infants."[21] As we have been discussing the issues of pollution, you might take a moment to reflect upon children's rights. Parents, policy makers, and corporations in the food and fuel indus-try all have a responsibility to provide an environment where children can thrive into healthy adults.

"For many children, dinner is served from a bag rushing between organized activities or sitting in front of a television. The meal itself composed of two pieces of white bread. Saturated and trans fats complete the meal. The meal is washed down with a sweetened high fructose corn syrup drink only to return to their activities on the computer or in front of the television to have a snack of chips and soda pop."[22]

Andrey Armyagov/Shutterstock.com

As we reflect upon the dangers of pollution on children, it becomes clear that children in utero throughout child-hood are dependent upon us as adults to protect them and offer them the opportunity to grow into healthy adults. We have been failing them by poisoning the food, water, and air. It's time to create a life for our chil-dren where they can play in nature, drink clean water, eat food free of pesticides and chemicals, and breathe air that supports the growth of oxygenated cells. We must choose life!

Photo courtesy of Maria Napoli

WAYS TO BUILD STRONG HEALTHY CHILDREN

- Feed them organic food
- Give them more water and drinks that are naturally flavored
- Offer them more free style play in the outdoors
- Keep the home chemical free
- Eliminate all processed sugar and caffeine
- Make sure they get enough sleep
- Ask questions to assure they are happy

- Spend more time playing and laughing with your children
- Reduce the time spent watching television and using the computer
- Listen to them, take their advice; they have knowledge too!
- Be mindful of their experiences and put yourself in their shoes

The sun, the moon and the stars would have disappeared long ago...had they happened to be within the reach of predatory human hands.

Havelock Ellis[23]

© Soloviova Liudmyla/Shutterstock.com

As you read about the importance of developing behaviors that support good health, you also need to be aware of how our planet is impacted by negligent human practices. Many are concerned about climate change and how it is effecting our communities. Although the earth's temperature has increased one degree since the late 1800s, the shocking news is that most of that increase has occurred over the past three decades! Rising sea levels, wildfires, heat waves, extreme storms and severe droughts are a few of the devastating effects of climate change. You might ask yourself, is climage change really that bad? Even a seemingly slight average temperature rise in enough to cause a dramatic transformation of our planet.[24] Remember how important oxygen is to our core existence. When we overload our atmosphere with carbon dioxide, trapping heat and raising the planet's temperature due to fossil fuels and deforestation, we are cutting our oxygen supply day by day. If we want to continue to not only survive on our planet but also do so in good health, there are some solutions you can begin to implement to decrease your carbon footprint. Reducing your carbon emissions by walking, car-pooling, driving fuel-efficient cars, and using mass transit. Live closer to work. Transportation is the second leading source of greenhouse gas emissions in the United States. Did you know that burning a single gallon of gasoline produces 20 pounds of CO_2!?[25] Breathing in carbon dioxide instead of oxygen will destroy your body one day at a time.

There is a sufficiency in the world for man's need but not for man's greed.

Mohandas K. Gandhi[26]

Simple changes can be made such as buying in bulk to prevent packaging, and using reusable grocery sacks, purchasing energy efficient appliances, and keeping lights off as well as appliances, television, stereos and battery chargers when not in use. Exploring renewable sources like solar, wind, geothermal, and bio-energy not only create clean energy and are being used worldwide but also are cost effective and create jobs for millions of people.[27] In support of your health and the environment, do not purchase products that use corn syrup and fructose, which requires barrels of oil for the fertilizer to grow it and diesel fuel to harvest and transport it.[28] Many of us are beginning to work at home, yet most of us are still spending most of our workday at the worksite, often 6–8 hours a day. When you take the time to have a pollutant-free workspace, you add quality to your life.

On a personal level, get involved. Educate your children, friends and family as well as tracking government officials who are making decisions about your health and future. Voice your concerns via social media or contact elected officials directly. You send a message that you care about the warming world.[29]

SOLUTIONS TO PROTECT YOUR WORK ENVIRONMENT

- Keep rest room sanitized by cleaning it regularly
- Provide adequate bath tissue, soap and paper towels
- Store cleaning supplies in a separate closet or cabinet from chemicals
- Keep the office kitchen clean from dirt and garbage by having sufficient trash receptacles and have them emptied daily
- Clean out refrigerators weekly
- Discourage staff from eating at their desks
- Look for water leakage and mold
- Keep a friendly attitude without judgment or harassment
- Encourage more people to use public transportation by offering free bus and light rail travel
- Bring a healthy lunch to work
- Eat with a friend
- Enjoy favorable conversations versus complaining
- Healthy Attitudes make work fun
- Take pride in your work

tobkatrina/Shutterstock.com

SOLUTIONS TO PROTECT YOUR COMMUNITY

- Choose a fuel-efficient vehicle for yourself
- Encourage public transportation to replace old buses with new ones that run on cleaner fuel
- Keep your engine tuned up and tires inflated
- Drive less and car pool more
- Choose renewable energy from wind, solar, and other clean sources
- Keep piles of papers off the floor to prevent fire
- Create more bicycle trails
- Plant more trees to increase shade and absorb CO_2
- Maintain health parks and forests
- Protect parks and forests from developers by getting involved in preservation activities
- Replace old public lighting with energy-efficient compact fluorescent light bulbs reducing carbon dioxide emissions (CO_2).

Photo courtesy of Maria Napoli

Now that we have discussed the issues and some of the solutions, you can begin to increase the quality of your health by living on a planet that was created to serve you. Our planet earth offers you the opportunity to breathe clean air with vegetation emitting oxygen and clean water to nourish your bodies. Sustain these blessings and live a long and healthy life!

LIFE DESIGN ENVIRONMENT CHECKLIST

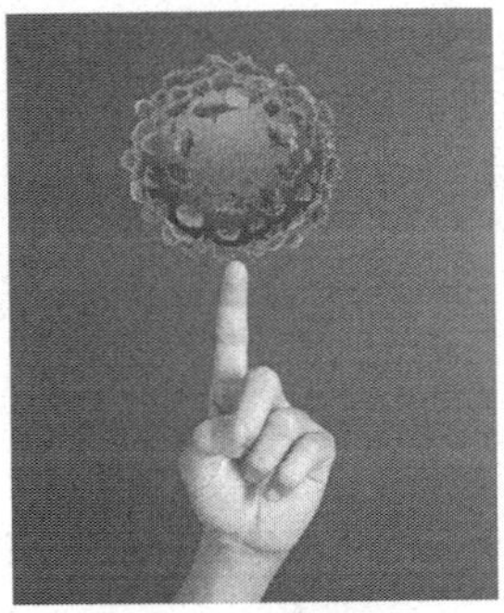

violetkaipa/Shutterstock.com

Things I need to do to check the air quality in my home:

Things I need to do to check the air quality in my workplace:

I know that the quality of the water I'm drinking is safe because:

I have walked through my house and have found:

These are my Three Strategies for being successful in creating change in my environment.

As you mindfully begin your designer activities, remember to use the Four Step MAC Guide as you remain present for all of your experiences.

MINDFULNESS PRACTICE
USING THE MINDFUL MAC GUIDE

Mindful MAC Guide

1. Mindfully **acknowledge** each experience without internal or external filters
2. Intentionally pay **attention** to your senses, thoughts, emotions, and instincts regarding each experience
3. **Accept** your experience without judgment or expectations
4. **Choose** to respond versus react to your experience

Discuss how well you did with your practice this week, feelings you had, obstacles you faced and how you overcame them.

_____

_____

_____

_____

_____

_____

_____

_____

_____

_____

_____

_____

_____

_____

_____

_____

_____

_____

_____

_____

_____

_____

DESIGNER ACTIVITIES

1. Go through all of you cabinets in your kitchen and pantry and take out everything that has chemicals or preservatives in it and write them all down. Then look up each of those chemicals and preservatives.

_____

_____

_____

2. Take a dry white cotton cloth and maybe a step stool. Swipe along your washer and dryer, stove, countertops, ceiling fans, patio door and window ledges, baseboards and air conditioning ducts. Now crawl on your floors, and if by chance you have a carpet, run your fingers through it and see what comes up.

_____

_____

_____

3. Take two glasses and fill one up with tap water and one with reverse osmosis or bottled water. Switch glasses around and without looking choose one and explore the taste, then taste the other. Notice.

_____

_____

_____

4. Soften your skin. Microwave or oven-warm a small bowl of olive oil. Kick back and soak your hands. Add some granulated sugar and scrub away the extra layer of dry skin that accumulated over the winter.

_____

_____

_____

5. Try an invigorating hand wash. Place a tiny bit of powdery ground mustard in a bowl with some other herbs and essential oils, such as rosemary and thyme or lavender and mint. Add hot water and wait for the tingling sensation of mustard to warm your skin.

_____

_____

_____

LIFE BY PERSONAL DESIGN
REFLECTIVE JOURNAL

In this Reflective Journal, record what you learned from this chapter, your "intentions" for change, any barriers you think might interfere with these desired changes and how you will overcome them, and at least *one* strategy that will help you realize your dreams and the life you will love.

_____

_____

_____

_____

_____

_____

_____

_____

_____

_____

_____

_____

_____

_____

_____

_____

_____

_____

_____

_____

_____

REFERENCES

1. Cornell University. (2007, August 14). Pollution causes 40 percent of death world wide, study finds. *Science Daily.* Retrieved April 10, 2011, from http://www.sciencedaily.com/releases/2007/08/07081362438.htm

2. Harper, H. A., Rodwell, V. W., & Mayes, P. A. (1977). *Review of Physiological Chemistry, 16th ed.* Los Altos, California: Lange Medical Publications.

3. http://www.quotery.com/authors/robert-orben/

4. Environmental Performance Report. (2001). http://www.tc.gc.ca/programs/environment/ems/epr2001/awareness.htm

5. Buttram, H. (2002). An appeal for clean air in the workplace: A Review of medical-legal issues surrounding the multiple chemical sensitivity syndromes. *Townsend Letter for Doctors and Patients.* August–September.

6. www.ewg.org *Environmental Working Group.*

7. Environ Health Perspectives. (2001). 109, 145–501.

8. http://www.infrared-sauna-reference.com

9. Ealy, H. (2011, October). The greatest energy always prevails: Interesting insights into advanced natural medicine. *No Limit Publishing.*

10. Environmental Protection agency. (2007).

11. Time Magazine. (2016, October 3). Household dust might be dangerous, 25.

12. Gunther, M. (2012). Our history, driving collaboration action on sustainability in the footwear, apparel, and home textiles supply chain. *Sustainable Apparel Coalition,* July 26.

13. http://www.msnbc.msn.com/id/23558785

14. Cornell University. (2007, August 14). Pollution causes 40 percent of death world wide, study finds. *Science Daily.* Retrieved April 10, 2011, from http://www.sciencedaily.com/releases/2007/08/07081362438.htm

15. http://www.msnbc.msn.com/id/23558785 Associated Press–September 08

16. Pesticides in the Food Supply Food Marketing Institute http://www.fmi.org/docs/media/bg/pests.pdf.

17. Ries, N. M., Rachul, C., & Caulfield, T. (2011). Newspaper reporting on legislative and policy interventions to address obesity: United States, Canada, and the United Kingdom. *Journal of Public Health Policy Vol 32,* 73–90.

18. http://www.cdc.gov/handwashing/when-how-handwashing.html

19. Louv, R. (2007). Leave no child inside. *Orion Magazine, March/April,* 4.

20. Bronstein, A. C., Spyker, D. A., Cantilena, L. R. M., Green, J. L., Rumack, B. H., & Giffin. (2010). Annual report of the American Association of Poison Control Centers' National Poison Data System (NPDS): 27th Annual Report *Clinical Toxicology* vol. 48 no. 10 2010.979–1178 2009.

21. Kalro, B. N. (2009, April). Vitamin D and the skeleton. *Alternative Therapies in Women's Health, 11 (4),* 25–32, 27.

22. Purcell, M. (2010). Raising healthy children: Moral and political responsibility for childhood obesity. *Journal of Public Health Policy 31 (4),* 433–446.

23. Ellis, Havelock. (1923). *The dance of life*. Boston/New York: Houghton Mifflin Company.

24. (2016) Global Warming Confronting the Realities of Climate Change. *Union of Concerned Scientists: Science for a healthy planet and safer world*. https://www.google.com/#q=Global+Warming+Confronting+the+Realities+of+Climate+Change.+Union+of+Concerned+Scientists:+Science+for+a+healthy+planet+and+safer+world

25. Biello, D. (2007). Ten solutions for climate change. *Scientific American, November 26.*

26. http://www.quotationspage.com/quote/38804.html

27. Conserve Energy Future. Global Warming Solutions http://www.conserve-energy-future.com/GlobalWarmingSolutions.php

28. Biello, D. (2007). Ten solutions for climate change. *Scientific American, November 26*

29. Denchak, M. (2016). How you can stop global warming: Healing the planet starts in your garage, in your kitchen and at your dining-room table. *Natural Resources Defense Council.*

CHAPTER 7

CHERISHING YOUR PASSIONS

© Pixel Embargo/Shutterstock.com

When work, commitment, and pleasure all become one and you
reach that deep well where passion lives, nothing is impossible.

(Unknown)

LEARN TO CHERISH YOUR PASSIONS

- Become introspective and self-aware
- Incorporate the practice of self-reflection into your daily life
- Look for ways to be joyful and happy
- Recognize and act on your passions
- Use the Mindful Four Step MAC Guide to cherish your passions

Passion is not something you think about or necessarily feel every day. Yet, when you consider the importance passion plays in your life, you may wonder why you don't think about it. Is it because you get caught up with just trying to live your life? Does passion get beaten down by other people or the "shoulds" they place on you and therefore it is forgotten? Is passion vulnerable to stressors, much like how stressors can stamp out joy? Or, does passion simply not enter your consciousness because you have not thought about it or it has yet to emerge?

Life without passion is like an ice cream sundae without whipped cream and a cherry on top. All you get is the taste of a cold substance but no delicious sweet joy or Technicolor pleasure.

Why is having passion so important? It is the unification of mind, body, and spirit. It is who you are; your inner desires, feelings, and dreams. It is what drives your core energy and ultimately, it is what gives you the strength to achieve fulfillment and success. How can you discover your passion? How can you draw out your inner desires, feelings, and dreams? The first step is to become self-aware and practice self-reflection.

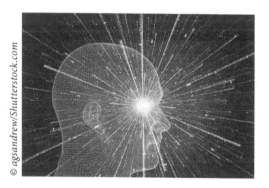

© agsandrew/Shutterstock.com

SELF-AWARENESS AND SELF-REFLECTION

When people are self-aware they are able to look deeply within themselves. They can think clearly about and understand their strengths, weaknesses, beliefs, emotions, and what motivates them to do the things they do. The positive outcomes of self-awareness is using what you know about yourself to control and shape your feelings and emotions (being emotionally intelligent), to set life goals, have direction, build strong abiding relationships, and make needed changes. People with high levels of self-awareness can almost "hear" their own thoughts. Conversely, when people are not self-aware, they have difficulty not only understanding themselves but also understanding others. They often make decisions with incomplete information or misdirected emotions and feelings, and then say and do things that can be interpreted as hurtful or uncaring.

The process of introspection is another way of talking about and looking at self-awareness. Introspection is examining one's conscious thoughts and feelings. Introspection is a helpful process for adults, in particular, and found to be useful for such groups as executives as a part of their leadership development; being objective, self-aware, and accurate leads to mature judgement and better decision making.[1]

Becoming self-aware is not something that happens easily or quickly. You have to decide that self-awareness is an important part of your life. It is then you can begin to look into yourself to self-observe and self-assess why you feel certain ways or act the way you do. For example, perhaps you find yourself very stressed and uncomfortable about a relationship you have. One approach would be to ignore your stress and feelings. Another would be to blame the other person for the way you feel. A third, and more productive approach, would to become self-aware—become curious about why you feel the way you do. You would literally stop to think about it and try to figure out what is "triggering" your stress and your feelings. Did something happen that reminded you of an experience in the past? What was said or done by this person triggered feelings of anger or sadness? Were you asked to do something unpleasant? These are just some of the questions you can begin to ask yourself to sort out what happened and why you feel the way you do.

Asking these questions in a positive way leads you to self-reflection. One source defines self-reflection as "the examination and contemplation of our thoughts and actions."[2] Another source shares that self-reflection is careful thought about your own behavior and beliefs.[3]

There are specific requirements to make self-reflection a regular part of life. These include:

1. Setting aside a routine time to self-reflect
2. Finding a comfortable and quiet place with no distractions
3. Using a specific set of questions to ask yourself
4. Being honest with yourself but also kind
5. Practicing mindfulness…not letting your mind wander
6. Using your breath to stay focused and calm

The following is a list of questions you can ask yourself to self-reflect. You don't need to ask them all. You don't need to write down your answers unless the act of writing them in a journal, for example, will help with your reflection. Select the questions you believe will be of greatest use in increasing your self-awareness. Realize the questions you ask yourself may change from reflection to reflection depending on your life situation.

- Whom do I see when I look in the mirror?
- What are my strengths?
- What areas do I need to develop?
- What do I value most in my life, work, relationships, and time investment?
- What skills do I have?
- What have been my achievements?
- What am I most proud of?
- What are my problems…what "baggage and skeletons" do I hold and bring to my life and relationships?
- How happy am I? Do I feel joy and gratitude and for what?
- How can I improve my life and relationships?
- How willing am I to change?

A recent study of nearly 150 male and female athletes found that self-reflection and self-insight were positively correlated with resilience. Self-insight, but not self-reflection, was negatively correlated with stress. The learning from this study and its importance was that self-awareness, and specifically self-insight, were able to lessen stress and promote resilience among these athletes.[4] A longitudinal study of over 200 nursing students was conducted to determine the impact of using self-reflection during their clinical practicum. The results revealed that self-reflection learning did improve their clinical competence and lowered their perceived practice stress.[5] These are just two examples of how self-awareness and self-reflection can not only improve the quality of your life but also promote resilience, help manage stress, and improve performance.

Another dimension of practicing self-awareness and self-reflection is to become your most authentic self with others. For many, this means becoming familiar with their many "selves." For instance, you may have one self at home, one at school, one at work, one who can become angry or sad, one who feels proud, one who feels fearful, and so on. Social Intelligence is a helpful model to understand your different selves and determine which of your selves you need to use to align well with the life you want to lead. Social intelligence includes as one of its skills, self-awareness which helps you navigate your interactions with the people and situations around you. It is called "street smarts" by some and tact by others.[6] For example, perhaps you are frustrated with your supervisor because she never gives you enough time at work to get your tasks completed. This frustration has now turned into anger. The anger is "authentic" and has caused you to begin disliking your job and the people you work with. However, by self-reflecting on the anger and being aware of it, rather than holding it in and being your "angry self" you realize the best course of action is to schedule a time to talk with your supervisor and find out how you can work through this problem together. You can still be yourself but you are able to use other means to handle feelings and emotions. Learning to be aware of who you are is critical to having emotional well-being. Interacting well with others will help you express yourself successfully.

RECOGNIZING YOUR PASSIONS

© EpicStockMedia/Shutterstock.com

Introspection, self-awareness, self-reflection, and social intelligence are just some of the dimensions of passion. Remember, passion is fueled by your thoughts and driven by your feelings and emotions. If you understand who you are, how you think, and reflect on how you act, you will begin to understand who you are and what you are capable of. But be aware you can feel deeply about something but not have the skill or the ability to make it happen. So, awareness of your thoughts, feelings, and emotions are the cornerstones to recognizing, embedding, and then engaging passion in your life. Therefore, passion is a state where energy is fully concentrated on a specific and all-important goal greater and more important than you are. It is an essential element to any worthwhile achievement.[7]

One other consideration of passion is how and when you feel attraction for yourself, others, and particular experiences. Since you have had unique life experiences you possess special desires, likes and dislikes that are unique to you and your life experience. These are important to consider. Do I like myself enough to pursue what is important to me? Am I attracted to others who help me build my life rather than stall it or tear it down? Do I put myself in situations that are healthy and growth producing or do I continually repeat experiences that are challenging, threatening, or self-defeating? Only you can decide if this is your pattern and how you set the "attraction meter" of your life.

Another perspective on passion is a conceptualization called the *Dualistic Model of Passion*. In this model, passion is aligned with activities. When there is passion there is a strong inclination to an activity a person likes, finds important, and is willing to invest time and energy. The dualistic nature of passion is expressed in the codification of passion. There is harmonious passion and obsessive passion. Harmonious passion is the internalization of passion as an activity in which the person has "free will" in determining engagement. That is, the passion for the activity is not overpowering but rather integrated into the person's life space. Conversely, obsessive passion is defined as leading a person to having an uncontrollable urge to engage in the activity. There is no "free will" but rather the passion itself drives the person to possible conflict and discomfort as decisions are made based on the passion as the "driver."[8]

A recent study of design students showed that harmonious passion was positively related to their creative achievement and provided a form of mediation between innovative cognitive style and creative achievement. However obsessive passion was not related to their creative achievement.[9] Another study looked at performance attainment of high school athletes and the *Dualistic Model of Passion*. It was hypothesized that both obsessive and harmonious passion would be positive predictors of deliberative practice and therefore positive predictors of performance. Harmonious passion was found to be beneficial in reaching high levels of performance as well as being related to a happy life. Obsessive passion was not as reliable in reaching performance attainment and was unrelated to happiness.[10]

This model provides an interesting premise regarding passion—harmonious passion or the internalization of passion appears to have a greater payoff when the nature of your passion is based on your "free will" and is an integrated part of your life.

Further research on passion found that "grit" (passion and perseverance for long term goals) can also predict positive outcomes.[11] Passion is also believe to have its own energy; observable and transferable. When people have passion they are able to overcome obstacles and find they have infinite potential.[12]

JOY, HAPPINESS, AND PASSION

*Joy is not a commodity to be hoarded and protected.
It is like a muscle. It must be used daily to keep strong
and vigorous. For all my hardships, I have been able to
remain quite joyful, for my muscles are strong.*

Source: Laura Moncur, *The Secret Heart of
Charlotte Lucas: More from Pride and Prejudice* (2014)

Passion also brings joy and joy is what makes life "worth living." Joy is what connects you to your deepest feelings and engages others to want to spend time with you. Joy is an ingredient of life often forgotten in the busyness of daily commitments. Joy leads to happiness and happiness is joyful. Sounds cyclic and it is. It is just the endless cycle you want to be in. Joy comes from your inner-self, and is connected to the source of life within you. It is caused by something really exceptional and satisfying. The source of joy is something or someone greatly appreciated or valued, and it is not only about oneself, but also about the contentment of those people whom you value the most. You can simply think about what makes you feel joy or be joyous. Is it the people you live or work with that brings that out in you? Is it the things you do? Is it where you live? Is it the pet you have that you can come home to at the end of the day who loves you only for who you are? Is it the goals or dreams you are currently seeking or those in the back of your mind that you know you need to get to? It may be any of these or other very personal and deep thoughts and emotions.

Closely related to joy is happiness; however happiness is external to you. Something can make you feel happy while joy is an internal process. Therefore, as you have probably found, happiness may be short lived while feeling a sense of joy can be long lasting.

© haveseen/Shutterstock.com

How do I achieve happiness? Well this can only happen if you want it to. Being emotionally happy means you see the world as a place in which you can be engaged in all the activities that appear "in front of you." Remember this is not an unconscious process. It is desired consciousness; being mindful of what is happening "in that moment." Does this mean everything is always wonderful? Not at all. It means that you find meaning in each aspect of your life.

The scientific study of what makes life worth living is "positive psychology." It underscores that what is good in life is as important as what may be bad.[13] Positive psychology is also about "valued subjective experiences." This includes well-being, contentment, satisfaction (with the past), hope and optimism (for the future), and flow and happiness (in the present).[14] There are three constituents of happiness: pleasure (positive emotion or being happy), engagement (gratification), and life meaning (a purpose in life). Happiness is about feeling good and it is you who makes the choice about whether and how much you want to be happy.[15, 16]

What is most significant about being happy is that research has found that happiness leads to desirable outcomes at school and at work and even to good health. And, that happiness can be taught.[17] Studies have shown that there is a "set point" for happiness, similar to a set point for weight. Therefore, some people who have a "high set point" do not have to work as hard—they are just happy! Further research on set points found that only 50% of happiness is determined by the set point itself with 10% attributed to life circumstance. This leaves 40% of the capacity for happiness within the power of a person to change.[18] More recently it has been found that happiness can be "hardwired." Studies reveal that the brain continues to reorganize itself throughout life by forming new neural connections, which makes it very resilient. A mechanism called, "axonal sprouting" occurs where undamaged axons grow new nerve endings to reconnect neurons whose links may have been injured or severed. Normal axons can also grow nerve endings and connect with other undamaged nerve cells and form new neural pathways. This allows for compensation in the brain for injuries or disease. This is called *neuroplasticity*. How does this work with happiness? When you use your mind to change your brain function and do this repeatedly (even for a short amount of time) you are changing

© Monkey Business Images/ Shutterstock.com

the strength of your neural connections. Just as learning a new skill, repeatedly feeling happy creates the activation of the neural networks, which is remembered and becomes "installed" in the brain. This cannot be done once. Rather, feeling happy must occur over a period of time to create the memory the brain can recognize for lasting change. This change is then stabilized and neural connections are strengthened. Happiness becomes a part of your mental state. Be aware that people usually tend to focus on the negative. Instead you want to be up front and present for your brain to have the "happiness hardwire" installation![19, 20]

There is an adage that happiness is not having what you want, but wanting what you have. It has been found that wanting what you have and having what you want accounts for happiness.[21] Recent Gallup-Healthways Well-Being Index (2014) results from a random survey of more than 175,000 Americans, ages 18 and older, who live in all 50 states and the District of Columbia, revealed that in 2014, 48.7% of Americans expressed happiness and enjoyment without a lot of stress. This is on the higher end of the happiness spectrum since 2008 with the exception of 2011 when it was slightly higher (49.1%). Stress and worry without happiness and enjoyment dropped slightly to 10.7%.

When queried about which days of the week they were the happiest, the response was weekend days (57% on Saturdays and 55% on Sundays). The weekdays were the least happy with Tuesday the lowest (44%) and not surprisingly Fridays higher (48%).[22]

Being happy is also thinking and talking happy. Thinking happy is being mindful. Being in the present allows you to be curious about your feelings. When negative emotions occur, they lose their impact because you are able to engage rather than react! Talking happy is finding ways to positively communicate with yourself and others. This means that sarcasm, cynicism, and negative self talk as well as being "mean spirited" are forms of communication that need to be put in your past. These communication patterns are not ones that are engaging nor are they singularly clear. For example being sarcastic is a form of communication that offers a double message to the other person. They are never sure if you are serious about what you are talking about and therefore the message itself is lost and the other person is left only with a feeling of potential anger, frustration, or perhaps feeling insignificant or hurt. So being able to "spin" messages to the upside and bring forward your happiness and joy is clearly a way to being endlessly happy. It is up to you!

ACTING ON YOUR PASSIONS

Identifying, igniting, and engaging your passion are important and make the difference between a "flat-line" life and one that is exciting, excellent, and is seen and felt as fulfilling and successful. The guide below provides the essential ingredients.

P = Perspective
A = Attitude
S = Sensitivity
S = Savor
I = Interest
O = Opportunity
N = Nourish

Examine your **PERSPECTIVE** about what life has been, is now, and what you would like it to be. Look back and then look forward. Use the strategies of meditation or dreaming what you would like to be, to do, to act on, or even attempt. Meditation and dreaming are free of charge and can be done whenever and wherever you like. You don't have to reserve them, pay for them, save for them, or ask someone else for them. You can meditate or dream a lot or a little. But you must first meditate or dream before you can "get in touch" with your passion.

Daily Affirmations

Reflect on your **ATTITUDE**. The attitude required for being passionate is adopting a positive approach to all that comes your way. Even when the "rain is falling" and you feel there is no end in sight, your attitude can help draw your passion. Passion cannot live and grow in a barren field. It must be nurtured with energy and strength and with an attitude filled with hope and desire.

Check your **SENSITIVITY**. Be sensitive to yourself and others. This leads you to understanding how you affect others and how they affect you. Your passion can be stalled if you have a "blind eye" to yourself and those around you. Use your skills of self-reflection to build the awareness you need to be self-aware about how you come across to others. The relationships you establish and maintain can be the barriers, or conversely, the promoters of your dreams and passion.

SAVOR each moment in your life. You have 1440 minutes each day. They go quickly and you cannot retrieve the ones that have passed. Be in the moment, breathe in, smell, taste, and appreciate every single one of them.

Cultivate your **INTEREST**. You have to be interested in pursuing what makes you feel passionate to engage in passionate activities. Without interest not much happens. Life becomes stale, bland, and filled with "white noise." Without interest you will not be able to draw enough energy to even think about passion. Become curious. Get interested in everything that comes your way because who knows, one of those interesting things that comes your way might just be the passion you were looking for.

Seek **OPPORTUNITY**. Every day there are multitudes of opportunities. The trick is being aware of them and not letting obstacles get in the way. If you have the ability to see them, you will find they will be staring you in the face. These opportunities are the avenues for you to ignite and engage in your passion. For example, say your passion is to write a book just like this one. You happen to mention this desire to a friend. The mentioning of the book becomes the opportunity because this friend has a colleague who publishes these types of books and can arrange an introduction. The opportunity led you down a tangible path to igniting and then engaging in your passion; writing the book. Simple!

NOURISH your passion. Make sure you focus on, think and dream about and then act on your passion each and every day. It is only through your continued energy will your passion stay lit. Give passion your attention and your intention.

Having passion is a necessity for a healthy, fulfilling, and successful life. It is a free commodity. Make haste. It is there waiting for you. You just have to look within and there it will be! It is one of the nicest ways to ensure you realize your dreams and live the *life you love*.

MINDFULNESS PRACTICE
USING THE MINDFUL MAC GUIDE

Mindful **MAC** Guide

The 4 Step MAC Guide will help you practice mindfulness.

1. Mindfully **acknowledge** each experience without internal or external filters

2. Intentionally pay **attention** to your senses, thoughts, emotions, and instincts regarding each experience

3. **Accept** your experience without judgment or expectations

4. **Choose** to respond versus react to your experience

Discuss how well you did with your practice this week, feelings you had, obstacles you faced and how you overcame them.

_____

_____

_____

_____

_____

_____

_____

_____

_____

_____

_____

_____

_____

_____

_____

_____

_____

_____

_____

_____

DESIGNER ACTIVITIES

Please answer the following:

1. What do you do, feel, think about, and/or act on that excites you?

_____

_____

_____

_____

_____

2. Describe what drives you to do positive things for yourself and others. List these and determine how often in a week you do them.

_____

_____

_____

_____

_____

3. What activities make you feel fulfilled and productive?

_____

_____

_____

_____

_____

4. Whom do you feel most passionate about? Why? How do these same people make you feel?

_____

_____

_____

_____

_____

5. Do you dream? If so, what do you typically dream about? What meaning do those dreams have?

_____

_____

_____

_____

_____

6. What was the last dream you had, whether awake or asleep? What was the dream and what was its significance to you?

© Yuganov Konstantin/
Shutterstock.com

_____

_____

_____

_____

_____

7. What dreams do you have that help you set your life goals?

_____

_____

_____

_____

_____

8. How often do you self-reflect? In what ways do you do this and how has it helped?

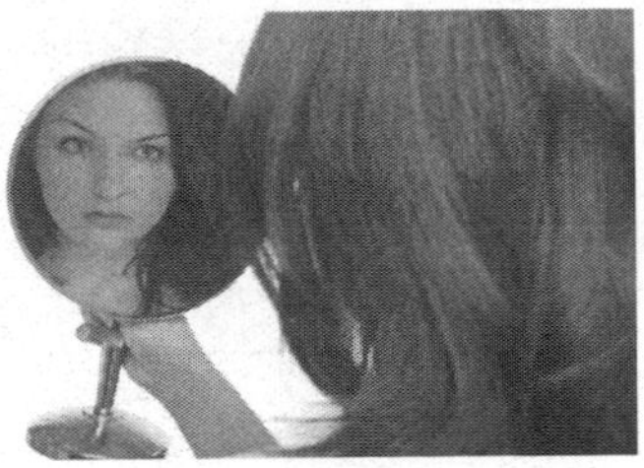
© Yuganov Konstantin/ Shutterstock.com

9. List the desires you have for your future. Describe how you might realize them.

10. What are your greatest joys? Do you experience these daily and if not, why? What would help you integrate these joys into your daily life?

11. Think about the last time you felt joy and also the last time you were completely happy. Describe your joy and the situation that made you feel completely happy.

_____

_____

_____

_____

_____

12. Find a photo of yourself or draw a picture of you when you were completely happy. Describe why you think this visual image represents your happiness.

_____

_____

_____

_____

_____

LIFE BY PERSONAL DESIGN
REFLECTIVE JOURNAL

In this Reflective Journal, record what you learned from this chapter, your "intentions" for change, any barriers you think might interfere with these desired changes and how you will overcome them, and at least *one* strategy that will help you realize your dreams and the life you will love.

_____

_____

_____

_____

_____

_____

_____

_____

_____

_____

_____

_____

_____

_____

_____

_____

_____

_____

_____

_____

_____

_____

READINGS OF INTEREST

Boniwell, I. (2012). *Positive psychology in a nutshell: The science of happiness.* Columbus, OH: Open University Press/ McGraw Hill.

Cassidy, G. (2000). *Discovering your passion: An intuitive search to find your purpose in life.* Westfield, NJ: Tomlyn Publishers.

Diener, D. (2008). *Happiness: Unlocking the mysteries of psychological wealth.* Hoboken, NJ: Wiley-Blackwell.

Duckworth, A. (2016). *Grit: The power of passion and perseverance.* New York: Simon & Schuster.

Gilbert. D. (2005). *Stumbling on happiness.* New York: Vintage Books.

Holahan, C. K., Holahan, C. J., Velazquez, K. E., & North, R. J. (2008). Longitudinal change in happiness during aging: The predictive role of positive expectancies. *International Journal of Aging and Human Development, 66*(3), 229–241.

Layard, R. (2005). *Happiness: Lessons from a new science.* Westminster, London: Penguin Press.

How to buy happiness. (2007). *Futurist, 41*(5), 6.

Ricard, M. (2007). *Happiness: A guide to developing life's most important skill.* Boston, MA: Little, Brown and Company.

Richardson, H. (1994). Proceed with passion. *Transportation & Distribution, 35*(4), 68.

Rubin, G. (2015). *The happiness project: Or, why I spent a year trying to sing in the morning, clean my closets, fight right, read Aristotle, and generally have more fun.* New York: Harper Paperbacks.

Self-fulfilling prophecies (2007, August). *University at Berkeley Wellness Letter, 23*(11), 8.

Seligman, M.E.P. (2004). *Authentic happiness: Using the new positive psychology to realize your potential for lasting fulfillment.* New York: Free Press/Simon and Schuster.

Seligman, M.E.P. (2006). *Learned optimism: How to change your mind and your life.* London: Vintage.

Sheldon, M., Kashdan, T. B., & Steger, M. F. (eds.) (2011). *Designing positive psychology: Taking stock and moving forward.* Oxford, England: Oxford University Press.

University of Pennsylvania. Authentic Happiness https://www.authentichappiness.sas.upenn.edu/

University of Pennsylvania. Positive Psychology Center http://ppc.sas.upenn.edu/

REFERENCES

1. Watts, G. W. (2012). The power of introspection for executive development. *Psychologist-Manager Journal, 15(3)*, 149–157.

2. Psychology Dictionary. What is Self-Reflection? Psychology Dictionary http://psychologydictionary.org/self-reflection/#ixzz4LwIjMQzR

3. Learner's Dictionary. Self-Reflection. http://www.learnersdictionary.com/definition/self-reflection

4. Cowden, R. G., & Meyer-Weitz, A. (2016). Self-reflection and self-insight predict resilience and stress in competitive tennis. *Social Behavior & Personality, 44(7)*, 1133–1149.

5. Pai, H. C. (2015). The effect of a self-reflection and insight program on the nursing competence of nursing students: A longitudinal study. (2015). *Journal of Professional Nursing, 31(5)*, 424–431.

6. Goleman, D. (2006). *Social intelligence: The new science of human relationships.* New York: Macmillan.

7. Comeau, R. (2010, December 21). Don't Cheat Yourself: Live with passion. http://www.articlesbase.com

8. Vallerand, R. J. (2010). On passion for life activities: The Dualistic Model of Passion. *Advances in Experimental Psychology, 42*, 97–193

9. Luh, D., & Lu, C. (2012). From cognitive style to creativity achievement: The mediating role of passion. *Psychology of Aesthetics, Creativity, and the Arts, 6(3)*, 282–288.

10. Valleranda, R. J., Mageauc, A. M., Elliot, A. J., Dumais, A., Demers, M., & Rousseaue, F. (2008). Passion and performance attainment in sport. *Psychology of Sport and Exercise, 9*, 373–392.

11. Duckworth, A. L., Peterson, C., Matthews, M. D., & Kelly, D. R. (2007). Grit: Perseverance and passion for long-term goals. *Journal of Personality and Social Psychology, 92(6)*, 1087–1101.

12. Norris, B. (2010). What is passion? Retrieved from http://briannorris.com

13. Peterson, C. (May 16, 2008). The good life. Positive psychology, and what it is not? Psychology Today. http://www.psychologytoday.com/

14. Seligman, M.E.P., & Csikszentmihalyi, M. (2000). Positive psychology. *American Psychologist, 55(1)*, 5–14.

15. Seligman, M.E.P., Parks, A. C., & Steen, T. (2004). A balanced psychology and a full life. *Philosophical Transactions of the Royal Society B, 359*, 1379–1381.

16. Seligman, M. (2011). *Flourish: A visionary new understanding of happiness and well-being.* New York: Free Press.

17. Peterson, C. (2008, May 16). The good life. Positive psychology, and what makes life worth living? *Psychology Today.* http://www.psychologytoday.com/

18. Lyubomirsky, S. (2008, May 4). How of happiness. The scientific pursuit of happiness. *Psychology Today.* http://www.psychologytoday.com

19. Hanson, R. (2013). *Hardwiring happiness: The new brain science of contentment, calm, and confidence.* USA: Harmony/Crown Publishing Group.

20. National Institutes of Health. Eunice Kennedy Shriver National Institute of Child Health and Human Development. Neuroplasticity. https://www.nichd.nih.gov/about/overview/50th/discoveries/Pages/neuroplasticity.aspx

21. Larsen, J. T., & McKibban, A. R. (2008). Is happiness having what you want, wanting what you have, or both? *Psychological Science, 19*(4), 371–377.

22. Gallup-Healthways Well-Being Index (2014). Happiness. http://www.well-beingindex.com/topic/happiness

CHAPTER 8

VISIONING YOUR LIFE

© PK9ix/Shutterstock.com

The future belongs to those who believe
in the beauty of their dreams

(Eleanor Roosevelt)

LEARN TO CREATE THE VISION OF YOUR LIFE

- Recognize the importance of having a life vision
- Determine where you fit in the Johari Window
- Assess your willingness to take risks
- Identify your values and priorities
- Appreciate how resilience and leadership impact your life vision
- Design your personal life vision statement and map or vision board
- Use the Mindful Four Step MAC Guide t0 create the vision of your life

THINKING ABOUT MY LIFE VISION

Personal life visioning and mapping is not typically something you stop and do or include in your daily activities. Yet these will have a great influence on how you conduct your life. Does your life seem controlled by other forces or people, or do you feel like you are in the center of a cyclone? Maybe you find yourself sitting on the outside of the world looking in? If any of these situations are occurring, then it is time for you to stop and begin to think about your personal life vision. Sounds easy, right? Well not really. It will take some time, thought, and your willingness to possibly take risks and set a clear intention.

Personal life visioning and mapping requires insight into all aspects of your life. Much of what we have discussed in *Life by Personal Design* has offered opportunities for you to become more aware

© Sergey Nivens/Shutterstock.com

of your own unique self and ways you can perceive and manage your life. Why is personal life visioning and mapping so important? Without a life vision you never have full understanding of yourself, as an individual, and the manner in which you want to conduct your life. Personal life visioning and mapping allows you to link your current and future life events with your life values and priorities, helps you make the kind of choices that can lead you to the *life you love*, and it offers you the ability to set goals and a personal action plan (your map) that incorporates your passion and your self-intentioned changes.

© vvita/Shutterstock.com

Although you may not be aware of it, visioning has always been an important part of your developmental growth. At each stage of your life you had some "vision" of what you might want to do next. Or, maybe somebody else had that vision for you and you went along with it because it seemed right or was convenient. However, these visions probably changed as you became an adult and your life experiences were integrated into daily, weekly, and yearly rhythms of who and what you are and how you conduct yourself individually and with others.

If you have never thought about your personal life vision, then the experience may be more daunting than if doing this is already a part of your life pattern. Don't let that stop you. Having a life vision and map can make a tremendous difference in your life. Remember, a life vision and map can change you from feeling out of control to a person who has not only a sense of direction but a set of goals that are being acted on.

One useful tool to use for personal visioning is the *Johari Window*. It provides a framework for understanding who you are and how you "fit" into your personal world. Developed by Joe Luft & Harry Ingham,[1,2] the Johari Window is a way to facilitate self-awareness, disclosure, and feedback.

THE JOHARI WINDOW MODEL		
	What others see or know	What others do *not see* or know
What I see or know	**1. The Public or Open Self**	**3. The Private or Hidden Self**
What I *do not* see or know	**2. The Blind Self**	**4. The Undiscovered Self**

The Johari Window represents feeling, experiences, views, attitudes, skills, intentions, and motivation that are framed in terms of whether the information is known or unknown by you, and whether the information is known or unknown by others. In the Johari Window, "self" refers to you and "others" refers to those people who are significant in your life (family, friends, work colleagues, etc.). The view is from four perspectives (or quadrants). They are:

1. **The public or open self is what is known by you and is also known by others.** This is the self you choose to share with others. For example, your friends may know a lot about you making your public or open self-quadrant quite large. But, when you meet a new person, the size of this quadrant may be small until you share more information about yourself. The aim is to always widen this quadrant. Because it is the public or open self where you are the most effective and productive—it should be free from mistrust, conflict, and misunderstanding.

2. **The blind self is what you do not know about yourself but is known by others.** These are things about you observed by others that you are not aware of. They can be positive or negative and can affect the way others act toward you. For example, you may have accidently gotten some food on your face when eating with a work colleague and are not aware of it, putting this information in your blind self-quadrant. If the work colleague tells you about the food on your face (gives you feedback), the information moves from the blind self to the public or open self-quadrant. If your work colleague is too embarrassed to tell you, the information will stay in your blind self-quadrant. The consequence of remaining there is that sometimes what others see and what you are blind to may cause untrue interpretations. Your colleague may think you are a sloppy eater. The aim is to always seek or solicit feedback from others to reduce the size of your blind self, making the open or public self-quadrant larger. Discovery is accomplished through the use of authentic communication and active listening.

3. **The private or hidden self is what you know about yourself but others do not know.** These are the thoughts or feelings you keep hidden from others for reasons that may include sensitivities, fears, or secrets. For example, you are able to play the piano but not well. You don't want your friends to know because they may ask you to play and you

would rather not so you keep this talent hidden. If you tell your friends, this information moves from your private or hidden self to the open or public quadrant. Typically, people are more open with those they trust. The aim is to disclose and expose relevant information, thus moving it from the private or hidden to the public or open self-quadrant. This promotes better understanding, cooperation, and trust, and reduces the potential for confusion, misunderstanding, and poor communication. The extent of the disclosure of personal feelings and information is up to you. Some people are more willing and able than others to disclose. Remember, always maintain your own personal sense of "safety" should you decide to disclose.

4. **The undiscovered self contains things no one knows about you—including yourself.** This may be because you've never exposed this area of yourself, or these things are buried deep in your subconscious. For example, you may have a natural ability or aptitude, but you are unaware of it, or you may have a fear but do not know its origin. A large undiscovered self-quadrant would typically be expected in younger people, and people who lack experience. Trying new things with no great pressure to succeed is a way to discover unknown abilities and reduce the undiscovered self-quadrant. As with disclosure and soliciting feedback, the process of self-discovery is very sensitive. The extent and depth to which you seek out discovery is up to you. Review chapter 7 to refresh yourself on self-awareness and self-reflection to remind yourself that these are two approaches to strengthen and deepen the discovery process.

The significance and impact of the Johari Window on your life comes in the ever widening and enlarging of your open or public self-quadrant, making the other three quadrants as small as possible. This is done by regular and honest exchange of feedback, and a willingness to disclose personal feelings. The examination of yourself through the use of the Johari Window allows you to understand what "makes you tick" and thus offers a platform for the creation and the maintenance of your personal vision and a resulting life map.

TAKING RISKS

Know that the process of personal visioning may be a risk for some. Why? Well, the reason is that what you may want to seek - your dreams and fondest desires—may be further out of reach than what may appear to be realistic or do-able at the present. But how will you know if you don't take the risk and try? When people take risks they are doing something that may involve personal or physical danger in order to achieve a goal.[3] With risk comes uncertainty.

For some, risk taking is very easy. In fact, some people thrive on risk. Think about stunt people in the movies or other thrill seekers. Risk is so pleasurable that to them it must always be incorporated into their daily lives. For many people, however, risk is calculated. Yet, for others it is a fear generator. In fact, some find they are risk aversive. These people experience physiological changes just thinking about risk and become desperately uncomfortable having intense feelings best described as unpleasant. Why does that happen? Risk taking challenges a variety of personal and professional "soft" zones that may include:

- Risk of failure
- Risk of embarrassment
- Risk of being hurt
- Risk of personal loss
- Risk of success

Too often people are willing to settle for the status quo because they believe something will more likely go wrong and overestimate what might happen if it does go wrong. This is called "catastrophizing." They may also go to the other extreme and underestimate their ability to handle the risk.[4]

Only those who risk going too far can possibly find out how far they can go

T.S. Eliot

Risk taking fears and anxieties may also be based on perception and/or cultural or learned barriers that may not be valid. Testing these is the key to moving forward. It has been found that truly successful people are willing to and are experienced in taking risks. They gather information about the risk itself and how the risk can be minimized, they set goals, and keep working toward those goals. They are patient and take action toward their goals after they have learned when they are more likely to achieve them, and see the future as a potential not to be avoided.[5]

So living life is about taking risks, and risks are needed to identify and realize your personal life vision. The first step in risk taking is just deciding that you are willing to risk. You must look at all of the options and alternatives and know that you need to move forward. The next step is examining what you value. Values are essential traits, qualities, and beliefs. They reflect your highest priorities and are deeply held.[6] Values are learned early and are influenced by those you are associated with as a child, and also by your friends, your experiences during school, what you read, as well as events both positive and negative during your work and adult personal life.

VALUES AND PRIORITIES

Values analysis is important because it allows you to find out what matters most to you. To determine your values, it is helpful to look at a list of values and mark which have the most meaning to you. Ranking them from your top to the bottom in importance to you is also extremely helpful. Some examples of values include teamwork, excitement, order, power, friendship, creativity, service, respect, honesty and so on. Once you have identified what you value, you can then set your priorities.

© Di Studio/Shutterstock.com

Your priorities can be difficult to set because many times the activities you need to be involved in compete with each other. Fulfilling these tasks may lead you to multi-tasking. Multi-tasking for many is very stressful and often not necessary. It usually occurs because priorities were not set. Priorities were not set often because your personal vision is unclear. That is, your life path and journey is clouded and your self-direction is muddled. To live your life with conscious priorities, try the following:

1. Take the time needed to determine what you want your priorities to be both at work, in school if appropriate, and in your life. Think about your values and also what and who is important to you. Then write down your top priorities.

2. Your tendency may be to write down many items. This is okay. But when you set them, choose two to three to really emphasize. If you have more, put them in a place where you can look at and perhaps act on them later. Keep things simple and focus on those priorities that make the most sense for your life right now and those you can truly give your attention to.

3. Every morning look at your list of life priorities. If appropriate include them in your schedule so your life actually reflects the priorities you have set.[7]

CL: Cartoonstock.com

"A great leader is a dealer in hope, Fenwick. Remember that."

RESILIENCE AND LEADERSHIP

Resilience and leadership are important as you begin to design your life vision and map. Why? Resilience is the ability to adapt to stressful situations without lasting difficulties. To do this you need to believe in yourself and have the capacity and strength to rise above adversity. This alone can give you a clearer view of your life vision. You are not knocked down by life but are invigorated by it.[8]

Resilience is not a group of traits or qualities rather it includes a person's thoughts, behaviors, and actions which can be learned. Do any of the "15 Factors of Resilience" describe you?

HOW RESILIENT ARE YOU?[9]

On a scale of 1–5, with 5 meaning that this best reflects you, rate yourself on the following **"15 Factors of Resilience"**

_____ Adaptable

_____ Aware of others

_____ Courageous

_____ Creative

_____ Flexible

_____ Have a sense of humor

_____ Have a sense of physical well being

_____ Optimistic

_____ Self Aware

_____ Self Motivated

_____ Self Reliant

_____ Spiritual

_____ Tough

_____ Value Driven

_____ Will Persevere

Reflect on the factors to which you gave yourself good ratings. How you can maintain those? Examine the ones with lower ratings. How you can strengthen your resilience? To do this, consider pursuing the following:[10]

- Look for opportunities for self-discovery
- Nurture a positive view of yourself
- Maintain a hopeful outlook
- Keep things in perspective
- Avoid seeing crises as insurmountable problems
- Accept that change is a part of living
- Move toward your goals
- Take decisive actions
- Take care of yourself

Finally, a recent study of resilience revealed that certain stressors can enhance the capacity for resilience. The researchers examined resilience-building or challenge stressors that provide opportunities for development of personal capacities in contrast to resilience-depleting (hindrance) stressors. The findings supported the study's proposal that challenge stressors indeed may create opportunities for resilience. Hindrance stressors depleted the capacity for resilience.[11]

Leadership is another important ingredient needed to help design your life vision. The definition of leadership relevant to this discussion is one by Warren Bennis: "Leadership is the capacity to translate vision into reality."[12]

This is essential. He goes on to say that leaders are self-aware and know their flaws as well as assets. Leaders are curious and risk-taking and also embrace errors to learn from them.

Today, the more accepted leadership theory and the one most relevant for looking at life vision is transformational leadership. The significant dimensions of this leadership approach for designing life vision is characterized by:[13]

- Intellectual stimulation—exploring new ways of doing things
- Individualized consideration—having open communication
- Inspirational motivation—communicating a clear vision
- Idealized influence—being a role model

While the focus of transformational leadership has been on followers, research was conducted to examine the benefits to leaders themselves. Across two experience sampling studies, it was found that subjects made a concerted effort daily to display behaviors reflective of transformational leadership (e.g., expressing enthusiasm and confidence, using vivid and inclusive language) and that these behaviors were associated with improvement in their affect by fulfilling their needs.[14] This study underscores the importance of suggestions and recommendations in this chapter about the importance of "seeing the world" from a positive perspective, having confidence to take risks, and incorporating the essential things and people into your vision all of which can lead to fulfillment of needs—leading the *life you love*.

DESIGNING YOUR LIFE VISION AND MAP

You are now ready to start designing your personal life vision and map to create the *life you love*. There are two parts to this process. One is your personal vision statement and the other is a map or vision board. The remaining information provides you with the design process.

Find a comfortable place to sit and think. If you like you can turn on your favorite music, or light a candle. Set up a relaxing environment. Breathe deeply and start reflecting on positive experiences in your life. You can use these questions to guide your thoughts. Don't forget to include the insights you had when you identified your passions in chapter 7.

- What are five things you most enjoy doing?
- What do you do daily to feel fulfilled?
- What are your four most important values?
- List three priorities based on your values.
- Write a goal for each of your priorities. These can be physical, spiritual, work or career, family, relationships, financial security, educational, or fun.
- If you never had to work another day, how would you spend your time?
- At the end of your life what will you regret not doing, seeing, or achieving?

Once you have reflected and answered these questions, you are ready to write a personal vision statement.

Be sure when you write your personal vision statement, it is written in the first person. It should be no longer than 50 words, action oriented, and anyone who reads it should be able to understand quickly and clearly where you are going and what you mean. Once it is completed you will use it to guide your map or vision board. Keep in mind that your personal vision statement can change over time, depending upon what is happening in your life.[15]

Based on the above, write your Personal Vision Statement

Personal Vision Statement of _____

The second part is creating your map or vision board. This is a visual illustration of who you are and the life you want to live. Use your personal vision statement to help you visualize and use any other thoughts or ideas you may have. Creativity is the key. There is nothing too big or crazy to add to your board. You want your board to be your very own unique interpretation. While you may want to create your board on your computer, a physical board is best.

Purchase or locate a poster or cork board in a size that seems right to you. You will also need glue, magazines, pins, and scissors. Look for magazines that have images that best represent what you want to "say" or illustrate. Cut and paste to your heart's content. You may want to go to a hobby or art store for stickers, colored paper, or other interesting materials. You can also use your own photos, either old or new, or even photo image databases. Some of these contain free images and others are subscription based. Add printed messages or written descriptions that you feel are appropriate to your vision. You can also include poems. Take your time as you search for what you would like to place on your board.

© Dean Drobot/Shutterstock.com

Tune into how the images and other materials are making you feel and do select or use only those that make you feel great. Don't look at the images in a traditional way. Move them around; turn them upside down. When you have all you want to place on your board, sit somewhere comfortable and review what you have. If you have a big pile of images that don't seem connected, don't worry they will start to sort out as you work on your board! ***Remember to feel not think during your design.***

When your board is finished, put it where you can see it. Look at it and think about how it makes you feel. Are you pleased with the outcome? If not, feel free to change what you have…paste over or add new images or writings. If you think it is not yet done, don't be frustrated. It is easy to add more at a later time.

Take a picture of your board so you can look at it whenever you want. Store the photo on your cellphone or laptop and take time during the day to look at it. It will help you stay directed. Enjoy the process as the risk is low and the payoff is high. When you are done you will be excited to see where you want to go and what you want to do.[16, 17]

Developing your personal vision statement and map or vision board is a culmination of all of the reading, reflecting, and activities you have completed as you have read through this book. Congratulations on reaching this important step in your journey to realize your dream and live the *life you love*.

MINDFULNESS PRACTICE
USING THE MINDFUL MAC GUIDE

Mindful **MAC** Guide

The 4 Step MAC Guide will help you practice mindfulness.

1. Mindfully **acknowledge** each experience without internal or external filters
2. Intentionally pay **attention** to your senses, thoughts, emotions, and instincts regarding each experience
3. **Accept** your experience without judgment or expectations
4. **Choose** to respond versus react to your experience

Discuss how well you did with your practice this week, feelings you had, obstacles you faced and how you overcame them.

_____

_____

_____

_____

_____

_____

_____

_____

_____

_____

_____

_____

_____

_____

_____

_____

_____

_____

_____

_____

DESIGNER ACTIVITIES

Please answer the following:

1. Think about yesterday. What was the most important activity you accomplished? How did you feel about that accomplishment?

_____

_____

_____

_____

_____

2. When you end your day, do you think about what you accomplished or did not accomplish or both? Or do you think about your day at all?

_____

_____

_____

_____

_____

3. If you never had to work, how would you spend your time?

_____

_____

_____

_____

_____

4. Reflect on what others have told you about your strengths and weaknesses. How did this make you feel? Did you make any changes based on this feedback?

_____

_____

_____

_____

_____

5. What risks have you taken in the last month? Were they new to you or ones you have tried before? What made it a risk for you? Does the level of risk stop you from trying to do what you desire? Why? What would help you take a risk?

_____

_____

_____

_____

_____

6. Think about looking at your personal vision statement and map or vision board three or six months from now. What changes do you think you might make? What areas might they be in?

After achieving his biggest accomplishment, Fido struggled to find a new sense of purpose to his life.

CL: Cartoonstock.com

_____

_____

_____

_____

_____

LIFE BY PERSONAL DESIGN
REFLECTIVE JOURNAL

In this Reflective Journal, record what you learned from this chapter, your "intentions" for change, any barriers you think might interfere with these desired changes and how you will overcome them, and at least *one* strategy that will help you realize your dreams and the life you will love.

_____

_____

_____

_____

_____

_____

_____

_____

_____

_____

_____

_____

_____

_____

_____

_____

_____

_____

_____

_____

_____

_____

_____

_____

_____

READINGS OF INTEREST

Crowley, M. C. (2011). *Lead from the heart: Transformational leadership for the 21ˢᵗ century.* Bloomington, IN: Balboa Press.

Goleman, D. (2011). *Leadership: The power of emotional intelligence.* Florence, MA: More than Sound.

Hansen, S. The Resilience Institute. http://resiliencei.com/

Southwick, S. N., & Charney, D. S. (2012). *Resilience: The science of mastering life's greatest challenges.* Cambridge, UK: Cambridge University Press.

Sullivan, D. (2006). *The laws of lifetime growth.* San Francisco: Berrett-Koehler Publishers.

Warrell, M. (2015). *Brave: 50 everyday acts of courage to thrive in work, love and life.* Hoboken, NJ: Wiley.

REFERENCES

1. Luft, J. (1969). *Of human interaction.* Palo Alto, CA: National Press.
2. Luft, J., & Ingham, H. (1955). The Johari Window, a graphic model of interpersonal awareness. *Proceedings of the Western Training Laboratory in Group Development.* Los Angeles: UCLA.
3. Merriam-Webster. http://www.merriam-webster.com/dictionary/risk-taking
4. Warrell, M. (2013, June 18). Take a risk: The odds are better than you think. *Forbes.* http://www.forbes.com/sites/margiewarrell/2013/06/18/take-a-risk-the-odds-are-better-than-you-think/#3e4bd1f21d09
5. Ewing, M. (2015, March 13). 5 risks highly successful people take. *Business Insider.* http://www.businessinsider.com/5-ways-successful-people-take-risks-2015-3
6. Heathfield, S. M. (2016, January 30). Identify and live your personal values for success. *The Balance.* http://humanresources.about.com/od/success/qt/values_s7.htm
7. Babauta, L. (2009, October 1). Setting priorities: Three mistakes to avoid. *Success.* http://www.success.com/article/setting-priorities
8. Resilience. *Psychology Today.* https://www.psychologytoday.com/basics/resilience
9. Roe, S. (2104). *15 Factors of Resilience.*
10. American Psychological Association. *The road to resilience.* http://www.apa.org/helpcenter/road-resilience.aspx
11. Crane, M. F., & Searle, B. J. (2016). Building resilience through exposure to stressors: The effects of challenges versus hindrances. *Journal of Occupational Health Psychology, 21*(4), 468–479.
12. Bennis, W. (2009). *On becoming a leader.* New York: Basic Books.
13. Bass, B.M., & Riggio, R.E. (2005). *Transformational leadership.* New York: Psychology Press.

14. Lanaj, K., Johnson, R. E., & Lee, S. M. (2015). Benefits of transformational behaviors for leaders: A daily investigation of leader behaviors and need fulfillment. *Journal of Applied Psychology, 101*(2), 237–251.

15. Heathfield, S. M. (2016, July 3). *Create your personal vision statement.* http://humanresources.about.com/od/success/a/personal_vision.htm?

16. Schwarz, J. (2009). *The vision board. The secret to an extraordinary life.* New York: Harper Collins Publishing.

17. Rider, E. (2015, March 14). The reason vision boards work and how to make one. *Huffington Post.* http://www.huffingtonpost.com/elizabeth-rider/the-scientific-reason-why_b_6392274.html

YOUR FUTURE CAN BE THE *LIFE YOU LOVE...*

You have now reached the end of the book, *Life by Personal Design: Realizing Your Dream*. But by no means have you ended your journey!

You are to be admired and congratulated for the advances you have made so far. The *life you love* and the dreams you have are there for you. You need to remain open and present to realize and appreciate the possibilities and opportunities. What we ask is that you continue to be mindful of yourself and your surroundings.

In closing, we have one more activity for you.

1. Revisit **Quality of Life Self Care Wheel - Reflection and Discovery** you completed at the beginning of the book.

2. Review each of the 7 dimensions and the ratings you gave yourself.

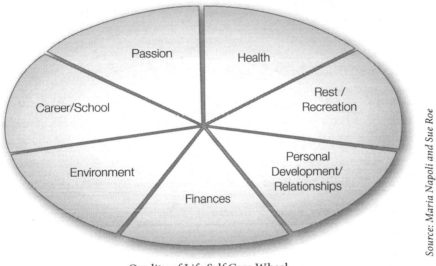

Quality of Life Self Care Wheel

Source: Maria Napoli and Sue Roe

3. Determine the reality of these ratings now. When you stated were you close to a 10 meaning you had fantastic balance and wellness? Or, were you closer to 5 or below meaning you needed to consider an adjustment in your life? How have these ratings changed? Feel free to cross out your ratings and insert the current ones so you can see your progress.

4. Also, review the work you did with **The 4 Step MAC Guide** and the *Life by Personal Design Reflective Journal* at the end of each chapter. Think about the changes you made as you moved from chapter to chapter.

5. You are now ready to complete the *Quality of Life Self Care Wheel—Plan for Intention and Action*. Input your current ratings. Review these ratings and determine an intention and one action you would like to take tomorrow to either maintain a high rating or work on a lower rating. What barriers do you think you will have to achieve the actions you set for yourself and what will you do to overcome them?

Quality of Life Self Care Wheel
Plan for Intention and Action

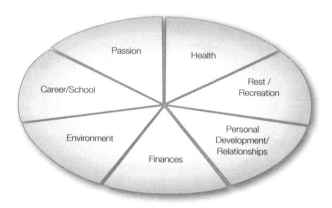

Instructions: Review your ratings and determine an intention and one action you would like to take tomorrow to either maintain a high rating or work on a lower rating.		
DIMENSION	**My Intention**	**My One Action for Tomorrow**
Health **Current Rating:** _____		
Rest/ Recreation **Current Rating:** _____		
Personal Development/Relationships **Current Rating:** _____		
Finances **Current Rating:** _____		
Environment **Current Rating:** _____		
Career/School **Current Rating:** _____		
Passion **Current Rating:** _____		

Source: Napoli, M., & Roe, S. (2017). *Life by personal design: Realizing your dream.* Dubuque, IA: Kendall Hunt.

To continue to pursue a life of quality and fulfillment, we invite you to reflect on and then write your overall intentions and actions for change for the next six months, for one year from now, and finally where will you be in three years?

Make your dream a reality. Give yourself the gift of the *life you love*…a Life by Personal Design!

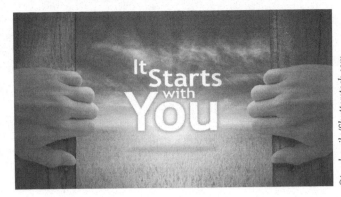

©tomkawila/Shutterstock.com